FORBIDDEN SANDS

Forbidden Sands

A SEARCH IN THE SAHARA

Richard Trench

ACADEMY
CHICAGO

First paperback edition 1982 Academy Chicago

Copyright © 1978 by Richard Trench

ACADEMY CHICAGO
425 N. Michigan Ave.
Chicago, IL 60611

Jacket: Sadic Wykeham

Library of Congress Cataloging in Publication Data

Trench, Richard.
    Forbidden sands.

    Reprint of the 1978 ed. published by J. Murray,
London.
    Includes index.
    1. Mali--Description and travel. 2. Sahara--
Description and travel. 3. Trench, Richard.
I. Title.
[DT551.2.T73 1980]   916.6'04   80-18580
ISBN 0-89733-028-5

ISBN 0-89733-027-7 paperback

TO MY FATHER

You . . . know there are those voyages that seem ordered for the illustration of life, that might stand for a symbol of existence.

Joseph Conrad, *Youth*

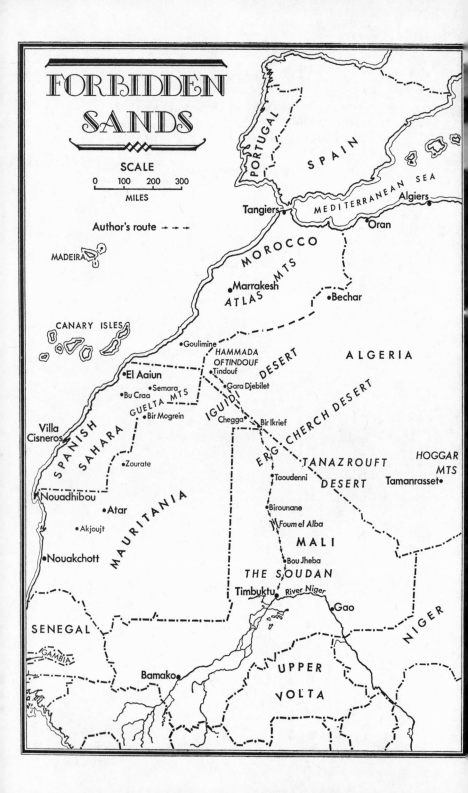

Contents

Acknowledgments

I would like to thank Oxford University Press
for permission to quote from *The Golden Trade
of the Moors* by E. W. Bovill.

R. T.

Illustrations

* The author's photographs

I

The Well at Chegga

As the heavy lorry lurched to a halt, the cloud of dust behind us was blown away in a sudden gust of wind. It was a hot dry day; only after the lorry stopped did you notice the wind. It blew across the desert in gusts, sweeping the debris of the day along with it as it went.

Directly in front of us was a granite escarpment. It stretched along the horizon for miles, completely obliterating the way ahead. On one side of it loomed a solitary headland that jutted out into the sand-sea, dwarfing an untidy gully strewn with boulders that lay on its left. At the entrance to the gully was a single water-hole, surrounded by a cluster of palm trees that spread themselves around it, bending like bows to the will of the wind. A few hundred yards away, further up the gully, three bedouin tents, half hidden behind the boulders, coughed and hiccuped in the breeze.

'This is the frontier, *Nasrani*,' the lorry driver said, using that despised term for strangers that the Arabs reserve exclusively for Christians. 'From here you go by camel.'

The driver stretched out his arm behind my neck and gave the sleeping nomad on the other side of me an unsympathetic shove. The fat man yawned, croaked, and spluttered into consciousness. Then, uttering a good-natured '*Bismellah*' (in the name of God), he hacked up a blob of phlegm and shot it out of the window, where it was quickly gobbled up in the dry sand. With his soul cleansed and his throat cleared he opened the cabin door and tried to get out. He couldn't. He tried hard, but it didn't work. The legs were too short and the trunk was too large. He stretched, he squeezed, he pushed, he pulled, but nothing happened. After a while he stopped his efforts, to rest and beseech the help of his god. Then, with unpredictable brutality, he gave a violent kick and rolled out. He ended up on his back in the sand, with his arms and legs in the air like a bad-tempered baby.

He got up, balancing himself on his insubstantial legs, and shaking himself down he summoned what dignity he could and waddled off to the back of the lorry. Sitting in the lorry's cabin, I heard him call out, in his harsh guttural voice, to the half-dozen hired hands perched on top, to come down and unload. I watched them through the lorry's side-mirror jump down and unload sacks, boxes, ropes, pack-saddles, waterskins, and all the other necessities for a camel caravan across the Sahara. I climbed out of the cabin to help.

'Go away, *Nasrani*,' the fat nomad shouted gruffly in Arabic. 'You are not wanted here. You will only get in the way.'

'He is nothing but a fat fool,' I thought, as I walked off feeling totally superfluous. I could not have been more wrong. I was the one who was to be the fool, it turned out.

That was the way it had been for three days, since we had driven off in a cloud of dust from the frontier town of Tindouf, an oasis at the top left-hand corner of the Sahara Desert.

We had left in the small hours, and by the time the pre-dawn half-light had emerged with its cold silvery mist, Tindouf and the century that it represented had disappeared far behind us. The dawn light was easy on the eyes, and the rising red glow in the east softened the bright austerity of sand and rocks.

Then the sun rose high above us, melting the colours of the desert into a single glaring tone that stayed with us all day, jarring our senses and blurring our horizons until evening, when it slipped down in the west and the harsh light gave way to that peculiar bluish-hue that always covers the desert in the early hours of night.

All along the route the landscape changed, from flat plains of gravel to neurotic outbursts of jagged rock, from slabs of jet black stone to carpets of coloured pebbles, from rounded breast-shaped dunes to skyscraping phallic buttes. The further we went into the desert, the more time seemed to slow down, until it stopped altogether and everything was as it always had been. I felt like a polluter from another planet. Even the dead were clean. The first camel I saw was a pattern of shining bones picked clean by the wind, its neck twisted in a dying agony.

We drove like that for three days, rising before dawn, stopping regularly for tea and prayers, and making our camp at dusk. And then on the third day, we came out of the range of sand-dunes, crossed a plain of gravel, and stopped in front of the high escarpment.

'This is the frontier, *Nasrani*,' the driver said.

I will always remember those words.

The place was called Chegga, or Ichig: a splash of fertile ground squashed between the Erg Iguidi and the Erg Cherch Deserts, close to where the frontiers of Algeria, Mauritania, and Mali meet. I paid little attention to Chegga at the time. It did not seem important. It was not the place that I wanted to go to, just somewhere on the way there.

The fat nomad was important. His name was Tahar Omar, sometime slave-dealer, smuggler, merchant, and now a caravan master; the proud owner of two houses, two wives, a transistor radio, and an Algerian passport. Among the nomads of the western Sahara he was an aristocrat. He came from one of Tindouf's old ruling families. For forty-one of his fifty-eight years he had taken camels across the Sahara. He knew where I wanted to go to, and for two hundred pounds he had agreed to take me there. At that very moment he was unloading stores for a caravan that would take me on the first part of a journey of nearly a thousand miles, through a place called Taoudenni to Timbuktu.

Timbuktu was not important. Since the Middle Ages Timbuktu has been a place of spectacularly little importance.

Taoudenni was important. Taoudenni is a concentration camp in the middle of the Sahara, a salt-pan mined, it was rumoured, by political prisoners and slaves. Few outsiders have ever been there, and those that have, have returned with the same condemnations.

'Taudenni', wrote the French geographer E. F. Gautier forty years ago, using one of its many varied spellings, 'is not fit for human habitation and the Negro workmen who are imported and held there by force, are killed off within a few years by its brackish waters. It is hardly possible that even under the most merciless regimes there has been an industrial hell comparable to this anywhere on the face of the earth.'[1]

The route to Taoudenni would take me south-east across the empty Erg Cherch Desert on to the Plain of Taghaza. From Taghaza we would swing south and come out on the salt-pan of Taoudenni. At Taoudenni I planned to change caravans and travel the second stage of my journey with a caravan of salt going to Timbuktu. The economy of Timbuktu is still based on the salt mined at Taoudenni.

That second stage would be no easier than the first. 'Centuries of traffic', wrote E. W. Bovill, the historian of the Sahara, 'have not lessened the dangers of the Taghaza–Timbuktu road. In 1805 a caravan of 2000 men and 1800 camels homebound from Timbuktu perished of thirst, not a man or beast being saved.'[2]

Those words were no exaggeration. The Taoudenni–Timbuktu road lay right along the length of the Tanezrouft Desert, a desert within a desert through which men race and never linger. 'Sterile to a degree that can hardly be found elsewhere', according to the French explorer Theodore Monod, 'so bare and flat that a stone, if there had been one, would have assumed the proportions of a mountain.'[3]

Suddenly the unloading of the lorry was interrupted by a shout from up in the gully. Everyone stopped to look. A knot of people had emerged from the tents and were coming towards us, waving their arms and calling out in welcome. They were led by a tall elderly man. He was loose-limbed and wiry, with a finely featured face. He was built like a thoroughbred and wore his beard like some ancient god, only more so. He walked quickly across the boulders, using the balls of his feet to spring from one stone to another. It was a body that did not only look as if it possessed great energy, but looked as if it possessed great resources of energy. His clothes and his turban were of indigo-blue. Over the years the blue dye had run out of the cloth, staining his chest, neck, face and beard, and giving him a distant, unearthly complexion.

[1] E. F. Gautier, *Sahara: The Great Desert*, Columbia University Press, 1935.
[2] E. W. Bovill, *The Golden Trade of the Moors*, Oxford, 1968.
[3] T. Monod, *Méharées, Explorations au vrai Sahara*, 1937.

Tahar Omar went up to the Blue Man and embraced him. The old man laid the palms of his hands on Omar's head, as nomad fathers do when they greet their sons, and pronounced the words of welcome.

'*Salam alaikum.*' Peace be with you.

'*Alaikum wa salam.*' Peace to you too.

'*Yak, la bas.*' No evil to you.

'*La bas.*' No evil.

'*La bas, Hamdullah.*' No evil, thanks to God.

And so it went on: the long, stylized exchange of ritual courtesies and veiled allusions that are the formal and traditional openings of conversation among nomads. Each line echoed by the other, like the chorus of an old song.

For each tribe in the Sahara the greeting is slightly different. A line is inserted here, another is taken out there. Normal conversation never begins until the unhurried greeting has run its course. This rigid structure is observed because it acts as a password separating friend from potential enemy, for a stranger will invariably falter over the lines. It is observed because it gives nomads meeting each other for the first time a chance to size each other up. And it is observed because it has always been observed.

When father and son had finished their greeting, the old man turned to me.

'*Salam alaikum,*' he said.

'*Alaikum wa salam,*' I replied.

The salutation continued for a few more lines. Then I faltered.

The old man asked his son who I was. Omar explained, referring to me always as '*el nasrani*', talking in a rough Arabic dialect that I could not understand. When the explanation was over, the old man beckoned me to follow him up to the tents. Two of the tents were his, he told me in simple schoolboy Arabic. He had two tents because he had two wives. One tent and two wives caused too much trouble, he explained. Spending alternate nights in each tent, he kept his 'trouble' to a minimum.

He led me to the tent of his elder wife, Tahar Omar's mother. She was a withered old lady, covered from head to foot in folds of black and looking like a bat. She had come out of her tent to see what her husband had brought back, and setting eyes on a *nasrani*—the first *nasrani* she had ever seen—she let out a squawk, flapped her arms about herself in panic, and flew off to the protection of her younger matrimonial rival.

The old man shrugged his shoulders and smiled apologetically as he led me into the abandoned tent. It was made up of blue rectangular patches that had faded in the sun. The patches had been sewn together and stretched out across a wooden frame made up of six uprights and two cross-pieces. Although it was spacious, about ten feet long and five feet across, it was very low, about five feet at the centre, and forced you into a permanent stoop. The tent was divided into two, one half for each sex. The female half was veiled off by a thick, brightly coloured blanket. A thickly woven rug covered the floor. The old man offered me a seat on it, and I made my way past piles of camel saddles, wooden chests, skins, sacks and rifles, to sit down in the middle. From there I watched Omar's father shoo away a squadron of flies, blow a smouldering fire to life, and set about making tea.

Tea-drinking, I soon discovered, was the pivot of desert existence. For hours the nomads would huddle together around their open fires, knocking back the tiny thumb-sized glasses of sweetened tea, uttering a '*Bismellah*' (in the name of God) followed by a '*Hamdullah*' (thanks be to God) with the same gusto that a whisky drinker might have exclaimed 'Cheers' ten years ago. A nomad's dependence on tea is not unlike a seasoned whisky drinker's dependence on alcohol. With tea inside him, he is capable of almost superhuman feats of endurance. Without it, he becomes a complaining wreck. 'Arab whisky', the camion driver had called it to me, showing off his cosmopolitan outlook.

As I drank tea with the old man, Omar came into the tent. The father handed him a glass.

'*Bismellah*,' the son said as he accepted it.

'I also have two wives and two houses,' he told me, not to be outdone by his father. 'One house and one wife is in Tindouf. The other house and other wife is in Timbuktu.'

He gave a self-satisfied little grunt. Evidently a house and a wife at either end of the Tindouf–Timbuktu caravan trail was not only convenient, it was good for business too.

'How many days will it be to get to Taoudenni?' I asked him

after a polite pause, still imagining myself to be living in the time-conscious twentieth century.

'Four days to Bouir Ikrief, *Inshallah*. Eight more days to Taghaza, *Inshallah*. And four more days to Taoudenni. Sixteen days in all, *Inshallah*.'

'When do we leave for Taoudenni?'

'When the camels arrive.'

'When will they arrive?'

'*Inshallah*.'

'?'

'The will of God,' he explained, pointing his finger up in the air and quoting the Koran. 'Do not say of anything that I shall do it tomorrow, say only that I shall do it when God wills it.'

'*Inshallah*', I quickly discovered, was the '*x*' factor in nomadic existence. It was the inexplicable variable that has always to be taken into account. The nomad's faith in God, his fatalism and his refusal to be drawn into anything definite, are all embraced by '*Inshallah*'.

'And when will it be God's will?' I rudely asked, not yet fully aware of the implications of the phrase.

'When will you stop asking pointless questions?'

Chegga, I began to realize, was important. Although at the time I was irritated by the delays and exasperated by the vagueness of it all, I am grateful for the time that I spent there. Oh, those days. Anxious days. Waiting days. Frustrating days. Yet they softened the shock of the sudden cultural change and took me across a frontier. Into another time, another place, another world.

My days at Chegga conformed to a regular pattern. I awoke each morning to the old man's call to prayer, winding its way into my sleepy consciousness, calling even me, who did not share their faith, to pray with them.

Allaho-akbar, Allaho-akbar, Allaho-akbar, Allaho-akbar
Ash-hado-allaa Ilaaha illallah, Ash-hado-allaa, Illaaha illallah
Ash-hado-ranna, Muhammad-ar-Rasoolullah, Ash-hado-ranna
Muhammad-ar-Rasoolullah
Hayya-ala-s-salah Hayya-ala-s-salah,

Hayya-ala-l-falah, Hayya-ala-l-falah
Assalaato Khairum mina-nnaum,
Allaho-akbar, Allaho-akbar La-Ilaha-illallah.

God is the Greatest, God is the Greatest, God is the Greatest,
   God is the Greatest.
I bear witness that there is none worthy of worship save God,
I bear witness that there is none worthy of worship save God.
I bear witness that Mohammed is the prophet of God,
I bear witness that Mohammed is the prophet of God.
Come to prayer, come to prayer.
Come to success, come to success.
Prayer is better than sleep.
God is the Greatest, God is the Greatest.
There is none worthy of worship save God.

Each line was repeated twice, the compelling words lingering over the still and silent camp as the soft music of the Gregorian chant once hung over the early morning fields of pre-Reformation England. The call to prayer brought together the believers in Chegga, young and old alike, who shivering in the cold and misty desert morning performed the *Wuza*, the washing of the body. They filled their cupped hands with water from a goatskin, drew it into their mouths and nostrils, and then lightly spread it over their arms and feet, repeating each action three times.

When the washing was over, they stood in two lines facing the east; the men and the youths in one line, and the women and children slightly behind them, divided by that unspoken and unquestioned sexual apartheid that so dominates life in the Islamic world.

'I have turned my face towards the Supreme Being, who has created heaven and earth, and I am not one of the polytheists,' intoned the old man who led the prayers.

'God is the Greatest,' the congregation replied, as they touched their ears and folded their hands over their chests.

'Glory to thee O God and blessed is Thy Name. Exalted is Thy Majesty. There is none to be worshipped besides thee.'

'I seek refuge with God from the accursed Satan.'

'In the name of God the Gracious and the Merciful. All praise belongs to God, God of all the worlds. The Gracious, the Merciful; Master of the Day of Judgement. Thee alone do we worship and Thee alone do we beseech for help. Guide us on the right path, the path of those upon whom Thou hast bestowed Thy blessing, not of those who have incurred Thy displeasure, nor of those who have gone astray. Amen.'

'Say He is God, the One God, the Independent and Besought by all. He begets not, nor was He begotten. And there is none like unto Him.'

The congregation bowed down three times, holding their knees with their hands and each time reciting 'God is the Greatest' and 'Glory to my God the Greatest'. Then the old man recited:

'Lord forgive me and have mercy upon me, and provide for me and make good my shortcomings and raise me up and grant me security and overlook my faults.'

'God is the Greatest.'

'All homage of the tongue, person and profession is due to God. Peace be on you O prophet and the mercy of God and His blessings. Peace be on us and the righteous servants of God. I bear witness that there is no God but Allah, and I bear witness that Muhammed is His servant and apostle.'

'O God, shower Thy mercy upon Mohammed as Thou hast showered Thy mercy upon Abraham and upon the true followers of both of them, for verily Thou art the Praiseworthy and the Lord of honour.

O Lord, vouchsafe unto us the good of this life and also of the next, and save us from the torments of Hell's fire.'

And so the prayer finished. Then the congregation turned to each other, first to the right and then to the left, saying 'Peace be on you and the Blessings of Allah', and bowing to each other as they said it.

Five times a day they prayed like that, their faces turned towards Mecca, as three hundred million other Moslems do, from the Malay Archipelago to the shores of the Atlantic, and uncounted generations have done before them, with a beauty and simplicity that has remained unchanged for thirteen hundred years.

For does not the Koran specifically state: 'Observe prayer at
the two ends of the day and at the hour of night in the proximity
of day' and 'recite the Koran at dawn'.

When prayers were over, the two lines of worshippers fragmented and the tiny community made their way to the tents for
the tea-ceremony.

I took my tea with Omar and his father, passing alternate
mornings in each tent, with tea, sugar, kettle, pot and thumb-
sized glasses laid out neatly before us. There was always silence,
a very primeval silence, when the old man struck flint against
steel and the smouldering rag, torn off his turban, grew into a
bush of flames, eating up the dried-up roots that the black-robed
women had collected the day before.

When the water had boiled it was poured into his silver pot,
with a measure of green tea and several hunks of sugar, and left
on a glowing bed of embers to stew. Then the old man would
raise the teapot high above his head and pour a thin column of
steaming tea into the glasses below and taste. If it tasted satisfactory, the old man would give thanks to God and hand round
the glasses. If it was unsatisfactory, he would screw his face
round his nose and add more sugar.

Three times he would go through these motions, three glasses
and three brews for each person. Why three? I never found out.
Once I asked Omar, but he just looked at me in disgust, shocked
at my ignorance. 'Because it has always been so,' he said. I might
just as well have asked him why the sun rose each morning.

No one ever hurried over the tea-ceremony. They dawdled
over the fire as if Time stood still while they drunk their tea. It
was often mid-morning before the group had fragmented, each
part splitting off to its separate task.

I spent my mornings with Omar, feeling bored, ill-at-ease and
self-conscious. He passed his mornings sitting cross-legged on
the sand surrounded by the baggage and merchandise that he was
taking on his caravan to Taoudenni.

As well as the essentials of nomadic survival, such as tea,
sugar and rice, all the shoddy trash of Europe seemed to have
washed itself up on those sands around him. There were Chinese
razors, plastic combs, cheap hair shampoo, sweets, chewing gum

sacks of blankets, boxes of toys and an encyclopaedia of other items. There was nothing hilarious about that fat man sitting there, mumbling away the Koran to himself as he went through his goods. He was no fool. He looked like some old tree, strong, domineering, reliable, and just a little eternal.

Although he could neither read nor write, he could add, subtract, divide and multiply at alarming speed. Sitting there in the sand he looked more Mongolian than Arab, with his tight, slanted eyes deeply embedded in his brutal, pock-marked face. The flabby folds of blue and bronze skin that flopped around him whenever he moved gave him the air of a potentate, a rough and brutal potentate with Mongolian blood in him.

But there was a loose, easy-going, somewhat complacent side to him as well. If I were ever to paint his portrait, I would do it in the style of the early Renaissance painters who wished to please their Italian lords. I would have him sit there in the sands and paint him surrounded by his world of razors, hair shampoo and pieces of chewing gum. And behind him I would have a string of camels waiting to be loaded. Such a picture would show him for what he was, the universal small-business-man, the head of a well-established transport firm that has remained in the family for many generations and kept financially solvent by constantly trekking the desert, between two worlds and countless centuries.

For a while he was content to have me sitting there beside him, watching him in silence. Then suddenly he turned on me aggressively in his blunt, uncompromising manner.

'Why do you come here?'

I was dumbfounded.

'What do you want from us?'

I could not speak.

'Why is it that you want to live like us? You who are a *nasrani* and rich. Why is it that you want to live like a poor man?'

'Because you are rich in other things,' I finally said, a little self-consciously.

He looked at me unsure. He must have suspected me of laughing at him. He was silent for a while, then his mood slowly changed.

'Your reasons are your reasons,' he said in pidgin Arabic that

I would understand. 'But do not forget that I know about you. I know the country that you come from. It is ruled by a woman. You cannot be a proper man,' he said, tapping his forehead with his index finger in that Moslem way that signifies intelligence. 'I have heard about your country on the radio. You cannot fool me. Ruled by a woman,' he snorted. 'Here you will have to change your ways, *Nasrani*. Here you do as we do.'

He looked at me roughly, and then, perhaps pitying me a little for coming from such a God-forsaken and woman-dominated country, he led me, patronizingly, towards a hobbled camel. 'I will teach you some of the ways of nomads and their camels,' he said to me, and began to explain the finer points of the camel. 'It has had three owners,' he went on, pointing to the three brand-marks on its neck.

'No,' I said, 'it has had four owners,' and I pointed my finger up to the sky to signify the fourth owner.

Tahar Omar's face cracked open with a smile. He slapped his hands hard against his flabby thighs and roared with laughter. 'You will do, *Inshallah*,' he said, tapping his forehead with his index finger again.

I found Omar's shifts from extremes of aggression and affection disquieting and disconcerting. Later I discovered that there was far more to these sudden changes than I realized at the time. Tahar Omar was playing a game of mental chess with me, to see which one of us would come out on top.

There is no such thing as an equal relationship among Saharan nomads. Society is a narrow ladder on which everyone has a place, and no two people share the same rung. In normal circumstances Tahar Omar would have had no difficulty in finding the correct place on his caravan for a passenger. But the presence of a *nasrani* made the circumstances highly abnormal. It complicated everything. On one hand, as a traveller who was undoubtedly rich (in Omar's eyes all *nasranis* were rich), my place was near the top of the ladder. On the other hand, as an unclean *nasrani* from a country ruled by a mere woman, I was lucky to find a place at all.

Tahar Omar never managed to solve this embarrassing social problem, and these early confrontations were never resolved satisfactorily for him. In the end my place on the ladder varied from day to day, depending on Omar's mood and on how far I matched up to his expectations. One thing that he never did was to make allowance for me as a stranger.

As well as Omar, his father and the two wives, there were the inhabitants of the third tent. Each evening they would troop up to the old man's fire, eat his food, listen to his son's radio, and study the weird *nasrani* who had appeared so suddenly in their lives. There was el Kiad, sharp-witted and fast-talking; his son Mohammed, who rarely spoke and seemed to spend most of his time caressing and cleaning his ancient bolt-action rifle; and there was 'Mood, who was waiting for his father and brother to turn up with the two camels that Omar needed for his caravan to Taoudenni.

El Kiad, Mohammed and 'Mood were all members of the war-like Rguibat tribe, 'the sons of the cloud'. Omar and his father were of the Tradjakant. For two hundred years the history of those two tribes has been one of perpetual conflict. Until the middle of the eighteenth century the Tradjakant ruled the western Sahara as firmly as the Tuareg ruled the central Sahara. Then in 1760 they were defeated by their neighbours, the Rguibat. The war that followed lasted for over two hundred years. As the economic cornerstone of the Tradjakants, the trans-Saharan caravan trade, began to decline, so their political and military power declined too. The Tradjakants were finally shattered at the Battle of Tindouf in 1896, when they suffered a crushing defeat at the hands of the Rguibat, a defeat from which they never recovered. From then on the Rguibat were the dominant tribe, indeed the largest, in the western Sahara, resisting the French administration until 1934, resisting the Spanish administration until 1958, and resisting the Moroccan administration today.

On my second day in Chegga, Omar, seeing me talking to el Kiad, drew me aside and warned me about the Rguibat. They were a dishonest and rascally crowd, he said, who were forever cadging and could never be trusted. The next day el Kiad gave me the same advice about the Tradjakant.

As well as the unscrupulous and untrustworthy inhabitants of the third tent, there were always visitors. The old man never withheld his hospitality. Apart from the tea, the food and the *nasrani,* the main attraction was Omar's radio. It droned away all night long, and the silent nomads listened to it with awe. These people had not yet come to take the radio for granted. To them it was still a mystery and a source of new and wonderful knowledge. With the arrival of the radio they had suddenly become aware of the world beyond the desert, and they marvelled at its size and diversity. They knew all about England and the B.B.C., whose broadcasts in Arabic they often listened to. They also knew about New York, Moscow, Peking and Palestine. *'Kissinger la bas'* (no evil to Kissinger), Omar exclaimed, after news came through on the radio of yet another Middle East peace mission. *'Kissinger Hamdullah'* (thank God for Kissinger) the other nomads nodded in chorus.

But it was the women, rather than the men, who dominated my attention, and particularly the old man's younger wife. She was in her early twenties, her face a lovely oval and her nose aquiline; veiled in black like a nun, with braided hair and silver bracelets, she had a refreshing beauty and an aura of sensuality about her.

Aware of that sensuality, she played with it, and played with me, letting her veil slip coquettishly, allowing a brief glimpse at some forbidden part, then retreating into coy and provocative giggles. She was more like a granddaughter than a wife to the old man. But the old man didn't mind. He was too old to mind, too old to care, and too old to notice.

Women of the Tradjakant tribe have far greater freedom than most Moslem women—although they have little enough all the same. Though the Tradjakant husband is absolute head of his household, he will never take an important decision without first consulting his wife, that is provided that she has already given him a male heir. Outside the tent the woman's position is subservient to the man's, but inside she is complete mistress of the household, with rights of property, privacy and separation. According to the American anthropologist Lloyd Cabot Briggs,[4] these rights are essentially pre-Islamic Berber concepts, thinly veiled behind Moslem law.

Yet in spite of the attraction of these women, I found them

[4] L. Cabot Briggs, *Tribes of the Sahara,* Oxford, 1960.

trying. They spent all their time mercilessly teasing me, trying to confuse me with their customs and imitating my ridiculous Arabic accent. They followed me everywhere, squawking with hysterics at everything I did. It was understandable. They had never seen a *nasrani* before. It was like theatre to them, only better, for the show was free and non-stop. At times I yearned to be alone, but there was little chance of that. I had about as much chance of privacy at Chegga as a Martian would have in London.

I will always remember those days at Chegga. They had a freshness and innocence about them, like first love. It was hard going trying to learn the ways of those people (ways as old as the world itself) and to fall into the rhythm of their lives. They were days of great mental strain. Everything was new, I was ignorant of their customs, and I found it easy to offend unwittingly.

'My mother is not like your women,' Omar screamed at me when I put out my hand to shake hers. 'Arab women are decent and self-respecting,' he went on.

Later, after he had cooled down, he explained to me that nomad women only shake hands with their own family. Outsiders, particularly *nasranis*, are expected to keep their distance.

Those days at Chegga! Each day ended at the point where it had begun, with prayers and a camp fire. When the sunset prayers were over, the nomads would gather together round the fire to watch the meal being cooked and listen to the radio. The menu was stark and simple: rice and dried camel meat. The cooking was simpler still. The mean-looking pieces of camel meat were soaked in cold water and then thrown into the cooking-pot with some oil, to fry. Rice and water would then follow. When the mixture, misleadingly termed '*el soupe*', had reached the correct density, it would be dolloped out into the communal eating bowl. The nomads would then wash their right hands, and after uttering the name of God they would dig into the mountainous meal with their right fingers. Arabs never use their left hand to eat with; they reserve that hand for cleaning themselves after having defecated.

It was a messy business for the inexperienced. Even if you manage to scoop out a handful of rice and meat and roll it into a ball using one set of fingers, you usually end up spilling it as you try to lob it into your mouth. Omar did his best not to look at me when I ate. He regarded my table manners as utterly appalling.

When the meal was over, everyone would burp out a 'Hamdullah', wash their hand again and sit in silent contentment. Although nomads have vast appetites, I never saw anyone at Chegga being deliberately greedy. Everyone was careful to have no more than his fair share, the fast eaters slowing down towards the end to allow the others to catch up.

Occasionally the menu varied when Omar baked bread. He would pour out flour from one of his many goatskin bags, dampen it, add yeast, and then pat it into a flat circular shape. Next he would rake out some embers from the fire and bury them in the ground with the uncooked loaf. He would wait until the bread rose, watching for the earth above it to come up into a mound, and then turn it over. When it was finally ready, Omar would take it out and break it into pieces for each person. The nomads would dunk it into a primitive stew of camel meat, exclaiming with delight on the goodness of the bread and the excellence of Omar's bakery techniques. I could not share in the appreciation of Omar's method. Sometimes the bread would be as hard as the stones we sat on, and at other times it would be as flabby as Omar's midriff.

Two things never varied in Omar's cooking. One was the sand that encrusted itself on everything that went into our mouths, and the other was the nature of the food. It was heavy, stodgy and wind-making. From my first meal on leaving Tindouf, I farted all the way to Timbuktu.

After the customary ten-minutes post-meal silence, we would either talk or continue listening to the radio. It was during these evening hours, watching my companions through the changing light of the camp fire, that I began to distinguish the individual faces from the flickering shadows, and to pick out the separate voices from above the drone of the radio. Everyone tried their best to talk to me in pidgin Arabic, but it was very hard. Conversation resembled that party game of guessing riddles, and moral judgements were reduced to the most basic: 'good' and 'not good'. I never stayed long trying to talk. The desert air, the attempts at conversation and the newness made me exhausted. After an hour I would unroll my sleeping bag and curl up into a deep slumber, oblivious to the voices, oblivious to the radio, and oblivious to the strangeness of it all.

On my third morning at Chegga, on my third glass of tea, Omar pointed to a line of tiny specks on the horizon. It was Dermas, his ex-slave, Dermas' son, Boyarek, and Omar's six camels. I strained my eyes but it was a full hour before I could distinguish the shapes of a man and a boy herding half a dozen camels towards us. They made their way slowly in the direction of the escarpment and began to climb up the gully. I could see them more clearly now. The man was a negro in his mid-thirties; he had closely cropped hair and a stubbly beard. Like the others he wore blue, the blue staining his dark skin and giving him a jet black complexion. Around his neck he wore verses of the Koran, like a St Christopher medallion, to protect him from evil spirits.

His son was about ten years old. Unlike the others who all wore sandals, he walked in bare feet. He was wearing a pair of white shorts and a brightly coloured, silk, Chinese kimono. How that piece of woman's clothing had escaped from a Parisian boudoir to end up in a nomad encampment in the Sahara is still a mystery to me.

Dermas and his son came up and hobbled the camels. With a silent flick of his wrist the father sent them off on a soft-shoe shuffle to some grazing by the water-hole. 'Salam alaikum,' Dermas said. 'Alaikum wa salam,' Omar replied, and the two of them went through the customary salutation. Then Dermas came up to the fire and sat down. He did not sit on a mat or a sheepskin as the others did. He sat on the ground a little apart from the rest of us. Slaves are not allowed to sit on their master's skins or mats, as freemen are.

The next morning Dermas and his son went off with the camels to a larger patch of grazing about two miles from the camp. They were to stay there, Omar told me, until Lehia, 'Mood's father, arrived with two more camels. I wanted to find out more about this semi-slave and his bizarrely dressed son, so I went with them to the patch of grazing, and stayed with them for several hours.

Dermas was a quiet man, unimpressed by the presence of a *nasrani* and with a simplicity and courtesy that I had rarely found among my own people. He had been officially liberated from slavery by the Algerian authorities over ten years earlier, but a piece of paper signed by a sous-préfet in Tindouf means little in the desert outside the frontiers of Algeria. Although he had been told that he was free, he did not consider himself to be free until he had bought his own freedom from his master, and since Omar gave him no wages but just the occasional tip, this would take a very long time. He held a position near the bottom of Omar's social ladder, but it was a position all the same. After his liberation, Dermas could have joined so many other displaced slaves in an unemployed half-life in one of the oasis towns under the protection of the Algerian authorities; but he was a nomad and he knew no other life than that of a nomad, so he decided to stay with Omar, a voluntary slave, but—as he told me—still a man.

Boyarek, his son, was in the same kind of position, but as a child he occupied an even lower position on Omar's ladder than his father. Soon, his father told me, he would be going to school in Tindouf. I found it hard to picture him in a classroom with class mates, knowing so much more about some things and so much less about others. He was a strange creature, with the experience and responsibilities of a man yet the years and the looks of a child, so I called him the Half-Child. Just as no allowance was made for me as a stranger, so no allowance was made for him as a child. Yet there were times when the child in him would come out; he would fall asleep, like Proust, listening to the sound of his own tears, and in the morning he would wake up with red eyes, his face lined with the salt stains of tears.

About mid-afternoon I decided to return to the encampment. The sky, normally so blue and translucent, had become yellow and dusty. The sun, usually so bright and flaming, had been reduced to an amber glow pushing its way through the dull yellow dust. No fear of sunstroke. The wind was breezy but nothing more. I said goodbye to Dermas and the Half-Child and began to retrace my steps. The longer I walked the duller the air became. Once out of sight of Dermas and his son, I could see no features, nor life, anywhere. Even the granite escarpment, so clear that morning, was now hidden behind the ominous dust.

Suddenly the wind begun to rise, blowing in short and powerful gusts; it increased in force until it had intensified into a gale. I looked around me. The surface of the desert, normally so still, was growing restless. As the wind rose, so the desert rose too. The ground was becoming vague and indefinable. It was dancing around my feet. The usually placid desert—that I had taken for granted as a landlubber takes the sea for granted—was gathering its fury and rising all about me.

It hurled itself against my calves, whirled around my body and beat at my bare arms. Nor did it stop there. It grabbed my neck, stung my face, encrusted itself in my throat, blocked my nostrils and blinded my eyes. I felt alone and feared death by drowning. I tried to stand firm to resist the impact of the battering wind, but I was blown over like a puff-ball of dust. I curled myself up with my face to the ground to find some protection in the ebb of the storm, but the sand gathered about me, piling itself against my rounded back and threatening to bury me.

I knew the direction of the escarpment and began to crawl towards it. It was torture to move, but it would have been masochism to have stayed still. As I crawled towards the escarpment I saw a shape on my left . . . a rock . . . a piece of vegetation . . . something to give me shelter. I made my way towards it on my hands and knees. I was almost on top of it by the time I saw what it was. Sand was piled high against its hump, its skin hung like parchment from its semi-exposed ribs, and its insides were swollen into vile and bloated shapes.

I crawled on while the wind and the sand roared about me, feeling my way like a blind man. By the time I reached the escarpment the tempest had calmed down. The air was still heavy with dust, but the ground was beginning to look firm again. The wind had dropped and the heavy particles of sand were floating down onto the desert floor in layers. For an immeasurable amount of time everything was very peaceful.

The following day Lehia arrived with his son Kahil, 'Mood's brother. They brought with them the two extra camels that were

needed for the journey to Taoudenni. They came in late afternoon from the north, Lehia leading the two camels and Kahil
next to him, carrying 'Mood's ancient and utterly useless rifle.
We were to leave the next morning, Omar told me. Lehia, Kahil,
'Mood, el Kiad, and Mohammed would ride with us for the first
few days, then Dermas, the Half-Child, Omar and myself would
continue to Taoudenni alone. All we had to do now was to wait
for Dermas and his son with the other six camels, expected the
next day, *Inshallah*.

I was glad to be leaving; for days I had been anxious to get off.
Try as I did, I found it hard to reconcile myself to God's will, and
like so many inexperienced travellers in Africa, I saw my journey
in terms of an airport timetable. I felt frustrated by the delays and
imagined, at times, that the entire Moslem world was plotting
against me. Besides, I was tired of the cadging, the curiosity and
the mockery, and—I forgot to mention—I had run out of
cigarettes.

While the others were making the preparations for departure,
I climbed up the escarpment to look out across the land that I
would be travelling over. All I could see was mile upon mile of
cracked, naked rocks and flat sand. Sand and rocks, rocks and
sand. It was a cracked and desolate region: timeless, spaceless,
and entirely dead. The monotony of it looked never ending and
the vastness looked frightening. It was alienating and remote,
far away from the strengths and comforts of living things and,
in spite of the heat, it looked terribly, terribly cold.

That night I dreamt of London. I was standing by a busy
main road with a pedestrian bridge across it. It looked like the
footbridge opposite Brixton tube station. The bridge was made
of scaffolding and was only half-built. I wanted to cross the main
road, but the cars were too many and they were going too fast. I
started to climb onto the scaffolding and I found that it was loose.
I started crawling along it, thinking that I would somehow
muddle across it. Ahead of me a section of scaffolding collapsed.
My friends in the street below were trying to persuade me to
come down, but I would not turn back. I was frightened of
looking a fool. I continued across the bridge. I got to the middle
and I could see the traffic roaring below me. Another part of the

scaffolding came down. I found that I could go neither forwards nor backwards; I was stuck. I wanted to call for help and come down, but my pride got the better of me. So I just stayed there in the middle until I woke up.

It is strange to recall now that I was surprised, indeed a little annoyed, when we did not leave the next day. Dermas never turned up with the camels. We waited all day but there was no sign of him. It never occurred to anyone to go and fetch him. He didn't arrive until nightfall and by then it was too late to leave anyway.

'We leave tomorrow, *Inshallah*,' said Omar, delegating the responsibility of departure to God.

That evening, while the others were listening to the radio, I took out my cheap Boy Scout's compass to study its workings. As I was examining it, Omar kept looking at me with barely concealed curiosity. Finally he could no longer restrain himself and he asked me what it was. I explained. He was silent for a while and then he spoke, pointing up to the North Star, or *Bel Hardi* as he called it.

'When I go from Chegga to Taoudenni I keep *Bel Hardi* behind my left ear. When I go from Timbuktu to Taoudenni I keep it in front of my nose. When I go from Chegga to Tindouf I keep it on my right eye. I do not need one of those things.'

'And the other stars?' I asked.

'They are no use. They always move around.'

I hardly slept that night. I was like a child on Christmas Eve waiting for the morrow.

The next day we did leave. We left because it was God's will that we should leave, or, in secular language, because Omar could find no more reasons for us not to leave.

Departure that morning took longer than expected. We passed an eternity sitting in one of the old man's tents drinking tea. As we drunk tea Omar explained to me the timetable for the days ahead.

'We will leave each morning at seven o'clock,' he said, indicating the position of the sun as others would indicate the hands on a wristwatch. 'We will walk for three hours and then we will ride for three hours. During the heat of the afternoon we will walk again so as not to tire the camels, and then we will ride until sunset.'

Like so many of his promises, Omar never kept this one. In the event he ended up riding most of the way to Taoudenni, and I ended up walking.

Finally the time came to load and leave. With sharp guttural cries the nomads heaved and hoisted the baggage onto the kneeling camels. As the camels were being loaded they snarled and bit at anyone who came within range of their twisting necks. With every piece of baggage put onto their humps, they roared and gurgled in protest, revealing throats somewhere in between a Florida swamp and the inside of a fig. To an outsider it looked like total chaos. There appeared to be no order anywhere. Yet there must have been method in that madness, although what that method was, I did not discover. It looked like a scene out of one of those nineteen-twenties silent film comedies. Loads were being lifted, nomads were shouting and camels were breaking free of their halters.

Halfway through the loading, Tahar Omar discovered that he was short of pack-saddles, so he ordered the Half-Child to make substitutes out of ropes and sacking. The first camel to be experimented upon with this makeshift pack-saddle bellowed so loudly that the camel next to him panicked and, breaking free from his rope, he galloped away. Everything was abandoned until the renegade camel could be captured. Finally he was brought under control by Dermas and the loading continued. But the camel who had started it all was still not prepared to accept the makeshift saddle. He fought back with fury. In the end four men had to sit on him while he was being loaded.

The hassle, hustle and bustle of loading continued. Camels were being beaten, dragged down and sat upon. Yet never once did I see unnecessary cruelty, nor did I ever see the needs of man come before the needs of the camel. There was no love between man and beast—after all, a nomad encampment is not a summer camp of the Pony Club of Great Britain—but there was a certain respect, an unspoken agreement between both parties that man would put the needs of the camel before his own needs, and that the camel in turn would deliver man to his destination, God willing. Respect, but not love. Love didn't come into it.

The loading was finally completed and the camels were dragged into line ready to go. They stood in resigned silence, waiting with bored disinterest. Loaded down and fully rigged, they looked a magnificent sight. Their long curved necks stood out like ship's bows. The riders' robes billowed in the wind like sails. The ropes that secured the camels' loads stretched across the animals like rigging. There is something in that term 'ship of the desert'. The Moors of the western Sahara still call the camel '*el Marhoob*', the ship.

As the camels stood to, ready to leave, two black buzzards encircled our encampment. 'They will bring us good luck,' Omar said, 'and follow us all the way to Taoudenni, *Inshallah*.'

Leading his camel, Omar begun to climb up the escarpment. The rest of us followed, and Omar's father, as old as a god, waved at us and wished us God's speed. It surprised me. My experience of God in Moslem countries was that He never hurried.

At the top of the escarpment I looked out across the plain of sand and rocks ahead of us. We mounted our camels while Mohammed and 'Mood, each carrying a rifle, took up positions on either flank. Then, just as we were about to go, a voice held us up. It was Omar. He was trying to mount his camel, a large white bull, while the Half-Child held its halter. Omar brought the camel down onto its knees and climbed onto it. But either Omar was too heavy or the camel was too stubborn. Either way the camel did not rise. Next he tried to mount the camel while it was standing up. But it didn't work. The legs were too short and the trunk was too large. He ended up hanging onto the camel's neck, kicking his legs around in the air like a bad-tempered baby again. Finally he called Dermas over. Dermas unmounted, bent over like a child playing leapfrog, and Omar climbed up onto his back, as if he were a mounting block.

Finally on top of his camel, Omar called out God's name and ordered the Half-Child forward. The little black boy gave the lead rope a tug and in one movement the caravan took a step forward in the general direction of Taoudenni. Omar dropped

c

his head and closed his eyes. He could not hope to see anything new on this caravan trek. He knew exactly what to expect. He had told me so himself. For two days we would be riding over alternate plains of sand and stones and slates and pebbles. After that we would cross a range of sand dunes and come onto another plain of pebbles that would take us to the water-hole of Bouir Ikrief (reputed to contain the best water on the Tindouf–Timbuktu caravan trail). From there we would march for two more days across sandy flatlands and rocky hills until we came to another range of sand dunes, far larger than the previous range. That would take us onto the Plain of Taghaza. From Taghaza we would swing south with *Bel Hardi* directly behind us until we arrived at the salt-pan of Taoudenni.

And so we were off. My dream had become a reality; I had discarded my old life like some useless out-grown coat. It was not quite the 'off' that I had expected, but it was an 'off' all the same. We must have looked an extraordinary sight. With two out-riders on either flank, we were trying to look fierce. But led by a Half-Child in a Chinese kimono, and commanded by a caravan master asleep on his camel like Humpty Dumpty on a dubious wall, we ended up just looking ridiculous.

2

The Way to the Frontier

We left for Taoudenni on 9 November 1974. I had been in Chegga
for five days. Yet the origins of that journey go further back,
eleven years back, to the steppe-lands of East Africa in the
summer of 1963. All my life I had lived in a city; it was my first
time out of Europe. I was frantic for experience and adventure.

My father was a District Commissioner in Kenya. His district,
which lay at the southern approach to the desert of the Northern
Frontier District, stretched out around the foothills of Mount
Kenya. Its townships were melting pots where negroes, Arabs,
Asiatics, Somalis and Europeans were thrown together, its
countryside teemed with wild game, and it lay bang on the
Equator.

It was August. Independence for Kenya was only a few months
away. My own attitude to that summer was confused. My mind
was cluttered with oversimplified and contradictory notions. On
one hand I knew that all empires were bad and that the Mau-Mau,
who had taken up arms against that Empire, were perfectly
justified. On the other hand my middle-class upbringing had
taught me that the British Empire was a fine and noble thing, and
that the Mau-Mau were nothing but half-educated savages.
Looking back in hindsight now, I agree with George Orwell that
while the British Empire could at times be bad and brutal, it was
far less bad and far less brutal than the younger empires that were
to follow it. I remember once asking my father what the Kenyans
thought about independence.

'The Blacks want it, of course they do.'

'And the others, the Somalis?'

He replied with a fatalist's shrug of the shoulder. 'If you ask a
Somali, he'll simply say, "We've had a white ruler replaced by a
black one".'

His reply confused me. Until then I had seen the world in terms of black and white, right and wrong. The shades of light that I now saw in the darkness and the shadows that I saw in the light sowed doubt in my mind and disturbed my notions of conventional wisdom.

Altogether I spent a month in Kenya. My father took me on two safaris. The first was by Land-Rover into the Northern Frontier District. We marvelled at leaping gazelle, felt shaken by herds of galloping zebra, confronted rhino, slowed down for elephants, peered at buffalo, and watched crocodiles bask in the dying sun. Yet in spite of the novelty it remained unsatisfactory and unfulfilling. Imprisoned in the Land-Rover I felt totally isolated from the world around me. There was no common experience, no point of contact. It might just as well have been cinema.

It was on the second safari, a shorter one of only two days, that I found what I was looking for. We drove by Land-Rover to an outlying district, mounted small tough-looking ponies and rode off with a patrol of mounted police. We came into a dark forest, zig-zagged down an almost vertical cliff—'Look, there are elephant droppings'—and drank goatsmilk at a Masai-Nderobo encampment. We rode all day, walking over great underground metropolises built by ants, trotting through herds of grazing giraffe and cantering with zebra at dusk.

That night we camped by a river stream. The crimson sun eased its grip over the ancient African day and my limbs ached. The desire for sleep had become a craving. I quickly faded into another world. When I awoke the next morning I was told that I had slept through the roaring of a dozen lions.

We left at dawnbreak along a dried-up river bed, over plains and up hills until finally, after breaking our way through parapet upon parapet of thorn trees, we reached the police post that marked our journey's end. I was exhausted. My bones ached, my thighs were torn, and my legs were a mass of blood. No matter. It had all been very short: a weekend trip, a polite non-violent razzia into the primitive, but it gave me what I had been looking for: a point of contact and a glimpse of what we had once been. The scorched neck, the tired bones, the short temper were not important. They were nothing but the price that had to be paid.

That journey left an indelible mark on my memory. In the years that followed, empty and barren years, the mental snapshots would return to me and I would see again the Masai-Nderobo warrior leaning on his spear, the sweating horses stretching their necks at the water-hole, the old lady with shrunken breasts holding out her hands in welcome. And as I saw those things I longed to return.

For eleven years I thought up possible journeys, drawing faint pencil marks on imaginary maps, planning vague timetables that came to nothing. I was in no hurry. The gaudy days of youth looked as if they had no end. I had no desire to cut short my endless strolling through early manhood. Then, after three years as a journalist in and out of Northern Ireland, I learnt that the present was only a flicker, and the future no more than a possibility. One night on a ferry to Liverpool, looking over the Irish Sea for the last time and feeling cynical and disillusioned at the physical and moral deaths of people who were close to me, I realized that I could no longer shelve my journey. I was in my mid-twenties. The regions of early youth were slipping behind me and I saw ahead that 'shadow line', as Conrad called it, beyond which the future becomes no more than a series of dull repetitions. I became haunted by the vision of myself as a middle-aged young man tortured by envy of the things I might have been.

'There are times', writes Graham Greene in *Journey Without Maps*, 'when we are less content to rest at the urban stage, when one is willing to suffer some discomfort for the chance of finding—there are a thousand names for it, "King Solomon's Mines", "the heart of darkness", if one is more romantically inclined, or more simply as Herr Heuser puts it in his African novel, *The Inner Journey*, "one's place in time", based on a knowledge not of one's present but of the past from which one has emerged.'[1]

I knew what I wanted, though I had no idea where I would find it. I had no intention of going back to Kenya. It would have been too déjà vu. I wanted to go further and deeper, to the simple

[1] Graham Greene, *Journey Without Maps*, London, 1936.

and the stark. I wanted to return to the very earliest of human
conditions, where I would be stripped of all levels of pretence, to
reveal myself for what I was, just as others would reveal themselves to be what they were. Such moments are rare in the Western
world; they come fleetingly, at times of revolution or great
national disaster. But I knew (from those days in Kenya) that in
those rare, raw and unrepentant regions left in the world, such
moments are the by-product of everyday life.

I first heard of Taoudenni by chance. I accidentally bumped into
a hashish smuggler whom I had known in those flower-powered
days of the late sixties. We went to a pub and talked about North
Africa and the politics of North Africa. He mentioned Taoudenni
in passing as an evil place with a name that had become synony-
mous with cruelty and fear in North Africa. I had never heard of
the place, but I wanted to find out more. But there was little
that he could tell me. The only thing he really knew about
Taoudenni was that it was a concentration camp in the middle of
the Sahara where prisoners were forced to mine salt. The country
that controlled it was called Mali, a black dictatorship that
stretched from the tropical rain forests of West Africa to the great
desert of North Africa; and Mali, Africa's answer to Papa Doc's
Haiti, did not encourage strangers.

'Have any strangers been there, to Taoudenni, I mean?'
'Oh yes. There was an American, a Frenchman and a German.'
'What happened to them?'
'The American was thrown into prison and nearly died before
his people got him out. The same thing happened to the French-
man. And no one even knew about the German until they let the
Frenchman loose.'

It was May 1974. As the summer went on, I became increasingly
obsessed with the idea of Taoudenni. Arab slaves and black
slavemasters: it was ironic; it was obscene. I searched for
Taoudenni on maps, but it was hard to find. Not only did each
map spell it a different way, but each map put it in a different
place. Like Kafka's Castle, it was not so much a place as a state of
mind.

I was determined to get there and find out about Taoudenni

for myself. Autumn and winter are the times for travelling in the Sahara and it was already early summer. Without a second thought I threw up my job, bought myself *Teach Yourself Arabic*, and began to prepare for the hard journey to Taoudenni.

I tried to get to Taoudenni the legal way. I stood in the early morning cold outside the Malian Embassy in Paris, ringing the doorbell that no one answered, waiting for the movement of the door that never opened.

'You will have to come back later,' a Moor from the Mauritanian Consulate on the other side of the courtyard told me. 'They always start their work later than everyone else.'

So I came back later. I filled in a form and tried to explain, but they just looked at me with bland uncomprehending looks and gave me another form to fill in. I ended up with a seven-day visa to visit Bamako, the capital.

I told them that I did not want to go to Bamako. They told me I would have to go to Bamako to get permission to go anywhere else, so it stood to reason that I should be given a visa to visit Bamako.

I knew perfectly well that the Malian government, God's gift to white racialists everywhere, would never allow a journalist to visit Taoudenni, so I gave up arguing and left with my seven-day visa. I was still determined to get to Taoudenni, more determined than ever before.

Bamako did not provide the only way to Taoudenni; there was another way, the illegal way. It was the same way that the American, the Frenchman and the German had taken, the camel's way. Taoudenni lay halfway down one of the oldest caravan routes in the Sahara, the Taghaza Road. I would simply turn up, suddenly and unexpectedly. If Taoudenni had anything to hide, then I wanted to take it by surprise.

The Taghaza Road began at Goulimine in southern Morocco, swung south-east through the Algerian frontier town of Tindouf, continued across the Iguidi and Erg Cherch Deserts, to the medieval salt-mines of Taghaza. From Taghaza it went due south to Taoudenni, and from Taoudenni south again, across the Tanezrouft Desert to the Soudan and Timbuktu. Not only was this route still used by camel caravans, but it offered me a perfect cover. I would play the loony Englishman with mad-dog ideas of crossing the Sahara by camel. I tested this cover story on my friends. They believed it, thinking that I was totally mad. It was just the reaction that I wanted.

I was elated. I would leave in the autumn. I spent the next three months laboriously trying to learn the rudiments of Arabic, fighting my way through the London rush hour to read about the Sahara in the British Museum, and building up my skinny, weedy body to an acceptable level of physical fitness. I even tried to give up smoking, but it didn't work.

Most of my friends regarded me as an unlucky victim of mid-summer madness, tactfully tolerating my obsession in the hope that it would pass away in the autumn. A few tried shock tactics to make me see sense. 'Why can't you just hitch-hike to India like everyone else?' one asked rhetorically. 'Nothing too serious to worry about,' I overheard another say, 'he'll just get stoned in Morocco and won't get any further.'

None of them knew about Taoudenni. I kept that to myself.

Of course everyone who heard about my mad-dog journey across the Sahara was quick to offer me the benefit of their advice, even those who most strongly disapproved of my plans. Someone in the British Museum told me to take plenty of books, a professional non-smoker told me I had a great opportunity to give it up, a Tory lady with a hat asked me if I knew anyone at 'the Embassy', a medical student gave me a list of drugs, a potential psychopath suggested I take a gun, and a do-it-yourself enthusiast insisted that I take plenty of string. I took everything except the gun and a desire to give up smoking, and I added to that list a totally ridiculous sheath knife of heroic proportions (for which I found no proper use except toasting Omar's bread), a series of maps (which I later found out were of the wrong places), a Boy Scout's compass (that I had no use for), and a sleeping bag with a puncture in it that left a trail of feathers all across the Sahara.

Did I take anything else with me? Not really. Courage? No, I didn't take that. I agree with Peter Fleming that it takes more courage to be a chartered accountant than an explorer.

Only one person offered me any really sensible advice: my

father. When I told him of my plans, he wrote back encouragingly, demanding neither explanation nor justification. 'Take two pairs of sandals and keep away from Tuareg women,' he wrote. It was the most sensible advice I received.

Imagine some ancient Moslem marabout sitting by his open tent with brooding black brows, bent over the Koran and contemplating heaven, completely at a loss as to what to take literally and what to take as poetic licence, and you will have some idea of me in the British Museum trying to learn about the Sahara.

'Around the Sahara is a region of wild beasts. . . . Beyond the wild beast region there is a tract which is wholly sand, very scant of water, and utterly and entirely desert,' wrote one respected chronicler.

The cornerstone of the Taghaza Road was the salt mine of Taghaza, and later of Taoudenni. From the eleventh century when Taghaza was first mentioned by Arab chroniclers until the middle of the nineteenth century, Arab merchants and travellers went south from Morocco, picked up salt at Taghaza and later at Taoudenni, and journeyed south again to Timbuktu where they exchanged the salt for gold and slaves. And from the books written by these Arab travellers we still have a picture of the Taghaza Road that has not changed until today.

Geographical knowledge was one of the richest branches of scholarship in the Moslem world. Making free use of Persian, Greek and Indian geographers, their travels made Marco Polo's journeys look like Sunday excursions. In 878 Abou Zeyed Hassan reached China and the Yellow Sea. In the same century his co-religionists travelled the length and breadth of India. In the Dark Ages the call of the Muezzin was heard in Cork Harbour. Two centuries later Ibn Fozlan journeyed through Russia until he reached a place where 'night was but an hour long'.

A desire for knowledge and a conviction that travel was a good character builder provided the justification for these epic journeys; trade provided the economic incentive. The Arab travellers had much in their favour. The once-in-a-lifetime pilgrimage to Mecca offered them a place where they could meet and exchange knowledge, their banking system stretched from one end of the Moslem world to the other, and all Moslems hold men who can read and write in great esteem. There was always a place on a caravan, a share in a meal, a door open for the Arab traveller. Are not Arabs famed for their hospitality?

Of all these travellers Ibn Battuta is probably the greatest. Born in Tangiers in 1304, he began his travelling career at the age of nineteen in 1325. After seeing most of the North African coast, he crossed the Sahara and travelled through equatorial Africa. In the journeys that followed, he visited Syria and the Levant, journeyed through Arabia, sailed along the East African coast, crossed the Hindu Kush, visited much of southern Russia, was shipwrecked in the South Seas, and saw the Great Wall of China.

It was on his second journey in Africa, begun in 1352, that he travelled down the Taghaza Road. He set off from Marrakesh on a diplomatic mission for the Sultan of Morocco, Abu Hassan; at Sijilmasa he stayed in the house of a man whose brother had offered him hospitality in China several years earlier. There he bought camels and provisions and left for Taghaza on 18 February 1352. It was a dry journey. The first water-hole that the caravan reached was empty, and Ibn Battuta nearly died of thirst. Two scouts went out to look for water. 'We found one of them dead under a scrub that grows in the sand; with his clothes on and a whip in his hands. The water was only about a mile away from him.'[2]

Ibn Battuta's 'takshift', or guide, was blind. It was not unusual for a blind 'takshift' to lead a caravan across the Sahara. A century and a half later, another great Arab geographer, Leo Africanus, writes of a blind guide who saved a lost caravan. 'He commanded some sand be given to him at every mile's end, by the smell thereof he declared the situation of the place.'[3] As recently as 1909, General Henri Gouraud met Mohammed ould (son of) Zouzoum, a blind man living at the Well of Char, whose profession was leading caravans through the Mauritanian Desert.

Ibn Battuta was not the only Arab traveller to pass down the Taghaza Road; there were thousands of them. Yet right up until

[2] Ibn Battuta, *Travels in Asia and Africa*, trans. H. A. R. Gibb, London, 1929.
[3] Leo Africanus, *History and Description of Africa*, trans. J. Pory and ed. R. Brown, London, 1896.

the early nineteenth century only one European, Anselm d'Isaloginers, a Frenchman, inevitably, is known to have crossed the Sahara. He left France in 1402, reached the River Niger and married a Songhai princess. He returned to France, crossing the desert, nine years later, with his wife, his child and six slaves. They arrived in Toulouse in 1413, and the nine of them settled down to a quiet provincial life. One of the slaves, a eunuch named Aben Ali, set up a medical practice based on black magic and bush medicines. Some years later, when the Dauphin Charles, later to be crowned king by Joan of Arc, fell ill in Toulouse, the eunuch Aben Ali cured him and was richly rewarded.

A hundred and fifty years later, a very different traveller was to make his way down the Taghaza Road. His name was al-Fasi, meaning the 'Man of Fez'. He is better known by his European name, Leo Africanus. Al-Fasi was captured by Christian corsairs off the coast of Tunisia in 1515. He was carrying on him the manuscript of a book, *The History and Description of Africa and the Noteable Things therein contained*. It was the account of two journeys he had made down the Taghaza Road. Instead of selling him into slavery, as was the custom, the pirates presented him to Leo the Tenth, the Medici pope, son of Lorenzo the Magnificent. Leo gave him a pension, arranged for his book to be translated into Italian, and renamed him Leo, after himself.

'As touching his exceeding Travels', wrote the English translator of the book, 'I have marvelled much how he should ever have escaped so many thousands of imminent dangers. How often he was in hazard to have become captive or to have his throat cut by the prancing Arabians or wild Moors? And how many times escaped he the lion's greedy mouth and the devouring jaws of the Crocodile.'[4]

Little is known of Leo Africanus before his capture ('For my own part when I heare the evil of Africans being spoken of, I will affirme my selfe to be one of Granada, and when I perceive the nation of Granada to be discommended, then I will professe my selfe to be an African.'[5]), and little has been heard of Arab geographers since. By the time Leo had had his book published, Christian merchants were sailing to India and China, trading on

4 *Ibid.*   5 *Ibid.*

the west African coast, and setting up gold mines in the New World. In geography, as in other branches of learning, Europe had not only caught up with the Moslem world, but had overtaken it. It is not by chance that Leo's book was published in Italian before it was published in Arabic. Leo Africanus is both the last of the great Arab geographers and one of the first great European ones.

While the British Museum provided me with acres of print about the Taghaza Road and the Arab geographers who travelled down it, its books told me next to nothing about Taoudenni. In 1828 an impoverished French adventurer, René Caillié, returned to Europe from Timbuktu along the Taghaza Road on a terrible journey in mid-summer, on which he nearly died. He was not the first European to reach Timbuktu (the first was a Scot, Major Gordon Laing, who got there two years earlier), but he was the first to come back alive, and the first to bring back accurate information about Taoudenni, which he heard about but did not actually visit.

These mines are the wealth of the country; they are worked by Negro slaves, superintended by Moors, who live entirely upon rice and millet, brought from Timbuctoo, and cooked with camel's flesh dried in the sun. The water which they drink filters through the salt, and is extremely brackish; to render it more palatable they put dokhnou (a drink made with millet) and honey into it; and they also improve this detestable beverage by mixing it with a sort of cheese reduced to powder, which I have mentioned above and which is nothing but curd dried in the sun.[6]

During the nineteenth century a succession of unsuccessful explorers tried to get to Timbuktu via the Taghaza Road. Perhaps the most extraordinary of these was John Davidson, son of a fashionable London tailor from Cork Street. Davidson had studied medicine at St George's Hospital and was a director of London's leading chemists, Savory and Moore. He was one of those rich Victorian eccentrics who litter the history of nineteenth-century exploration. Before trying to cross the

[6] René Caillié, *Travels through Central Africa to Timbuctoo*, London, 1830.

Sahara, he had travelled extensively over Asia and North
America, collecting a great deal of quasi-scientific information
which was no use to anyone. In the 1820s he caused a scandal
among the armchair explorers of London by publicly unveiling
an Egyptian mummy before the Royal Society.

Davidson believed that a trip to Timbuktu via the Taghaza
Road would be the crown of his achievements. He urged his
influential friends to bully Lord Palmerston into putting the
frigate H.M.S. *Scorpion* at his disposal. He secured letters of
introduction to the 'King of Timbuktu' from various unimportant members of the British nobility. And then with the freed
slave Edward Donellan, who claimed to have been born in the
city (Davidson tested Donellan's authenticity by confronting
him with a hippopotamus in the London Zoo), he embarked at
Falmouth on 3 September 1834 on an expedition to Timbuktu.

Poor pathetic Davidson! Nothing went right. There were
delays at Algeciras and setbacks in the Maghreb. In December
1835 he was still in Morocco. 'I had hoped to be in Timbuktu by
this time,' he wrote on Christmas Day.[7]

He could never understand the deviousness of the natives. The
flies, the dirt and the slavery made him sick. He became the
reluctant guest of the Sultan of Morocco. 'As I am unfortunately
to live at the Sultan's expense, it will cost about four times as
much as if I had to buy everything,' he wrote on 13 January.
Besides the continual 'bakhshish' to be handed out, he was
constantly in demand as a doctor. The Sultan asked him to make
a check-up on his wives and concubines—all two hundred and
fifty of them; next he asked Davidson to examine all his eunuchs;
and the number of women who told him that they were carrying
dead children in their wombs almost drove him to distraction.
'Oh, that I can get away. Never was I so sick of any place as this.
I am literally worn out.'

By the end of April he still had not left. How easy it appeared
in theory: 'Sok Assa is distant only one day's journey; Tatta
four; Akka five; Todeny twenty; from this to Arowan is another
twenty and thence to Timbuktu seven'. How hard it was in
practice.

[7] John Davidson, *Notes Taken During Travels in Africa*, London, 1839.

By May he was finally at the edge of the desert. 'No one knows where we are to go,' he wrote sadly. The Tradjakant were in the middle of their hundred-year war with the Rguibat and there were no caravans leaving for Taoudenni. Davidson was so desperate that he offered to buy the entire stock of Taoudenni salt and give it to the caravan master who would take him to Timbuktu. It was no use. The local merchants suspected him of being a spy or, even worse, a trader trying to by-pass the Arab middlemen.

There is something sad and a little heroic in John Davidson's last letter to his brother. 'Before this reaches you, I shall be wending my way over Africa's burning sands to a sort of fame or the sad "bourne from which no traveller returns". . . . Think sometimes of the poor lost wanderer.'

He finally set out on 5 November from Wadnoon. His interpreter had abandoned him, and except for his companion, Edward Donellan, he was alone and ill. Thirty-three days later he was killed by Tradjakant tribesmen at Chegga, just five days short of his thirty-ninth birthday. Edward Donellan found a caravan and continued on to his home at Timbuktu. Nothing has been heard of him since.

In 1880 a German, Oscar Lenz, visited Taoudenni on his way to Timbuktu. He was the first European ever to visit the mines. He left Morocco, passing through Tindouf, where he saw a column of Bambara slaves, and continued on to Taoudenni. At Taoudenni he planned to pick up a caravan of salt and continue down to Timbuktu. But when he got to the mines he found them deserted, presumably due to the non-arrival of the caravan that was to bring the miners their provisions, so he continued on to the Soudan without any provisions, nearly dying.

Lenz was another typical nineteenth-century globe-trotter, a racialist, an imperialist, ridiculously brave and extremely charming. In spite of the lack of water he insisted on a daily shave. He was loath to allow his standards of hygiene to deteriorate. 'I was never able to persuade myself to give up using white sheets during my journey. I continued doing so until the end,' he wrote in his book.[8]

[8] Oscar Lenz, *Timbuktu*, Leipzig, 1884.

After visiting Timbuktu, he decided to return to Europe via Dakar. He arrived in Senegal in rags. The first French officer whom he encountered was so astonished at his tramp-like appearance that he almost turned Lenz back. 'This coat may be old but it was made in Paris,' Lenz told him.

That was virtually all that I could find out about Taoudenni. Twentieth-century history about the salt mine was as scanty as nineteenth-century history. In 1906 the French Army built a military post there, but they were forced to abandon it. In 1911 the entire population of the salt mine perished because the caravan that was bringing them provisions was delayed in a sandstorm. The French finally managed to build a post there but they were unable to stop slavery. After all, who but slaves would work such mines? In the 1930s the French newspaper *Le Monde* reported that slaves were still being used at Taoudenni; in the 1950s an American who visited the mines reported that the miners were being held in debt-bondage; and in the 1960s rumour had it that the newly-independent Mali had turned the salt mines into a concentration camp to house her Marxist and Tuareg political dissenters. Since then nothing has been known of Taoudenni, except that there was an American, a Frenchman and a German.

Soon it was September, and time to leave. Surrounded by the denim legions of the American Express weighed down by surf boards and rucksacks, I boarded the night train at Victoria Station and set off for Paris. I arrived at the Gard du Nord the next morning.

In Paris I discovered that all the expensive maps that I had brought with me were of the wrong places. I made a dash by Metro to the offices of the Institut Géographique National, but it had closed. In the end I had to content myself with a Michelin tourist map of North and West Africa, which I bought from a news-stand at the railway station.

On the train travelling through Spain, the sun boring through the carriage window, I read a strange and haunting book: Helen Waddell's *Lives of the Desert Fathers*. In the book Cassian, a desert mystic, writes of a madness that comes at midday.

It is akin to dejection and especially felt by wandering monks and solitaries, a persistent and obnoxious enemy of such as dwell in the desert, disturbing the monk especially about midday, like a fever mounting at a regular time, bringing its brightest tide of inflammation at definite accustomed hours to the sick soul. And so some of the Fathers declare it to be the demon of noontide which is spoken of in the XCth Psalm.

[Such moments are] beyond sound of voice or movement of the tongue or any uttered word, when the mind is narrowed by no human speech. . . . Towards eleven o'clock or midday it induces such lassitude of body and craving for food, as one might feel after the exhaustion of a long journey and hard toil, . . . one's mind is an irrational confusion, like the earth befogged in a mist.[9]

Richard Burton once remarked that there are three starts to every journey in Africa: the first start, the long start, and the real start. My first start began in Morocco, where I first set eyes upon 'the Splendour and the Havoc of the East'. From Tangiers I took a bus to Marrakesh to meet a man called 'Robertson' (that's not his real name). Robertson was a coral trader. He took cheap watches and transistor radios down to the Saharan tribesmen and swapped them for precious coral stones that he could sell in London at several hundred per cent profit. 'Robertson' knew the Sahara, my dope smuggling friend told me. He had been told that I was coming, and he could tell me a thing or two about Taoudenni. On my train journey through France and Spain I had begun to build up 'Robertson' in my mind. He could give me reliable information about Taoudenni; he would get me on a caravan to Taoudenni; he would 'fix-it'.

I arrived in Marrakesh in the early morning, and made my way through a labyrinth of streets until I got to the house where Robertson was supposed to live. I found him stoned out of his mind, a state that he seemed to have been drifting around in for several weeks. He was lying on a mat in the shade. When I came in he looked at me and vaguely waved. He didn't even have the energy to get up. His girl-friend was in no better state. She had

[9] Helen Waddell, *Lives of the Desert Fathers*, London, 1936.

turned up in Marrakesh on her way to Europe from Australia, and had got no further. She was suffering from severe hepatitis but couldn't even 'get it together' to go to a doctor. She kicked a half-starved cat off a rug and offered me a seat. The cat miaowed pathetically and then ran away. She offered me a joint but I refused it. I had more important things to do than get stoned.

'Caravans?' said Robertson. '*Walloh*. Nothing.' He was like one of those second-hand Somerset Maugham characters, using the occasional native word to impress the newcomer.

'Does that mean that there are no caravans across the Sahara?'

'None from Morocco. The King is making claims on the Spanish Sahara. He hopes to divert the people away from complaints about the way he runs things here, and thinks that a great anti-colonial crusade led by him will do it.'

Robertson was right. All over Morocco, in newspapers, on the radio and on hoardings, the King's message of 'Liberation' of the Sahara was being pumped into the apathetic minds of his subjects.

'Will this last a long time?'

'He's trying to revive the old Moroccan Empire under the guise of liberating a handful of tribesmen from the "chains of Spanish fascism". The Algerians know the game he is playing and will try to stop him. They might succeed. The tribes in Spanish Sahara like the Algerians but they hate the Moroccans. They don't like having to pay up "bakhshish". Now Hassan's arming his own border tribes and claiming that they are Spanish Saharan rebels. The Algerians are worried about the fears of an invasion of the Sahara, and the Spanish are flying more troops into the territory. There'll be a full-scale war.'

Robertson had retreated into a stoned haze. I tried to find out more from him but all I could get was vague and contradictory. The only thing that was certain was that the road to Taoudenni and Timbuktu from Goulimine was closed, and that all caravan traffic from Morocco had ceased. So ended the first start.

I looked at my Michelin map. The next major oasis after Goulimine was Tindouf, on the western border of Algeria. So instead of stopping to rest and leave the details of it all to the will of God, as any experienced traveller would have done, I

D

grabbed a succession of buses, trains and lorries back into
northern Morocco, across the border into Algeria, and then down
through Algeria to Tindouf. That was the long start.

I arrived in Tindouf a week later after a series of minor delays
too petty to go into. It was the middle of September. I trudged
down the dry and dusty streets looking for the town's only café,
weighed down by my books, my medicines, my knife, compass,
sleeping bag, and two pairs of sandals, all tangled up in string.
At the café I made enquiries about caravans to Timbuktu.

'Oh no. There are no caravans leaving here. Don't you know
the date? It is the beginning of Ramadan. There will be no
caravans for at least a month.'

I laughed with relief at the ridiculousness of it all. I had done
everything to prepare myself . . . everything except look at the
calendar.

There was nothing for me to do but return to Morocco. I
could not stay in Tindouf for a month. In a town so charged with
tension because of the Spanish Sahara I would have stood out and
invited suspicion. Tindouf was bound to be overcrowded with
spies and informers, and I had no desire to advertise my presence
to the Malian authorities so early in my journey. So I decided to
return to Morocco, where I could disappear in the crowds of
hippy holidaymakers until Ramadan was over. The long start
had been as unsuccessful as the first start.

A month later I returned to Tindouf. Tindouf is a frontier town
and with the crisis in the Spanish Sahara it was being rapidly
turned into an armed camp. Olive-clad soldiers jostled with
blue-clothed tribesmen in the market-place. There were rumours
of the desert tribes being armed, guns being shipped across the
border, and there was talk of raids. As I came into the town, a
patrol of the Algerian Camelry Corps was riding back to base.
Tindouf had not been captured by the French until 1935. It was
the last place in the Sahara, probably one of the last places in the
world, to be pacified, and in October 1974 it was once again a
wild and uncertain place. The very word 'Tindouf' means
'frontier post' or 'centre for guarding'.

On my third day in Tindouf I was met by two frontier police-men. They wanted to know what I was doing there. I told them I was looking for a caravan and kept it vague. They left and came back half an hour later. I was to be taken to be questioned by the Sous-Préfet, they said.

I was taken by Land-Rover to the Sous-Préfet's office. As we drove up, an elderly gatekeeper made an ineffectual effort to get up and then sank back into a half-sleep. Outside the office, some forty shouting and jabbering petitioners were queuing up. As the Land-Rover came to a halt, all forty turned their heads, staring silently at me with still glassy eyes, like soldiers responding to some silent command. Walking past them with the two police-men, I heard one man mutter the name 'nasrani' (Christian). It was the first time that I had heard that word, a word that for three months was to be the only name that I was known by.

The main door of the office opened and out of it hopped one of those strange hybrid creatures so familiar to the Third World yet so totally unknown to Western Europe. He wore a yellow turban and a slightly crumpled white linen suit. His tie was well askew and very tight, keeping in place a nervous face that sported a big black moustache and a pair of unshaven cheeks. He had a club-foot which he dragged down the steps after him as he bumped along towards us. He was some sort of government clerk, I suppose, but his official position did not really matter. He was a little man and, like so many other little men before him, he compensated for his littleness in stature with bigness in power. He had worked for the government since the year dot and knew everything that happened in Tindouf; where everyone lived and exactly what they were doing at any given moment. If any local government can ever be said to have a soul, he was Tindouf's soul. Wherever he went he was surrounded by a posse of petitioners. As he came down to meet us, the petitioners fell on him en masse. He shooed them away with dignity and ushered us into the building.

I found myself standing in a large imposing office. On one side of the room was an empty mahogany desk. Behind the desk were rows of books and maps. They were not the usual kind of books that you would expect to find in a government office on the edge of the Sahara: government reports and anthropological studies on 'the natives'. There was a complete works of Voltaire, a book by Diderot, a French edition of Shakespeare, books by Marx and Engels, works by Sartre, some plays by Bernard Shaw, and a couple of Franz Fanon.

As I studied the room, I heard an educated voice behind me speaking in French.

'You are probably wondering if you are under arrest or if you have been invited to tea?'

'Yes,' I said.

'Will you take some tea?'

The man speaking was plump and middle-aged. His well-cut Parisian suit discreetly held back nearly half a century of paunch. His head was as polished as his mahogany desk, and his skin was as brown as the old leather on his books. He indicated a low-lying table with tea glasses and sweetcakes on it.

'I imagine that you want to go to Timbuktu?'

I smiled and nodded, like a child caught out by a grown-up.

'By camel, I imagine?'

'By camel.'

'Other people, when they want to go somewhere, are happy to go by aeroplane, or at least by car. But not the English. They always want to go by camel.'

I was silent. In a strange way I was enjoying the gentle mockery of this mysterious man.

'. . . and I, who like the idea of adventure, will be very pleased to help you. I am a great admirer of the English.'

Like all Arabs, he was a great flatterer.

He told me that the Taghaza Road was hardly used now. Most of the water-holes had dried up. Occasionally nomads did use it, however, especially if they were going to Taoudenni, since no lorry went there from Algeria. He was silent for a while and then he turned to me. He just happened to know of a nomad who was going there in early November. He asked me if I was interested.

'Yes.'

He summoned his government clerk and sent him off in search of the nomad.

'What will this caravan carry?' I asked after the clerk had left.

'Anything. Tea. Sugar. Contraband.'

Contraband. That interested me.

'What kind of contraband?'

'Guns, radios, kief.'

'Kief!'

'My dear friend, they make their fortune out of it.'

A moment later there was a knock at the door. It opened, and if you had been there, you would have wanted to laugh. An obese bedouin was trying to squeeze through the door, but the government clerk was wedged in next to him, and the nomad could not move. His legs were too short and his body was too large. Finally he took a deep breath, gave the clerk a push and shot him through the door, the fat nomad rolling in after him.

'Monsieur l'Anglais,' said the Sous-Préfet, 'may I present to you Monsieur Tahar Omar.'

Tahar Omar could not speak French, or so he said. So the Sous-Préfet had to act as a translator. But it was obvious that Tahar Omar was not entirely ignorant of French. At the mention of money, a responsive smile came over his face.

After several minutes of dialogue Tahar Omar agreed to take me, so long as I paid the right price. But setting a 'right price' was no easy matter. With the nomad working on the assumption that all *nasranis* are rich, and the *nasrani* working on the assumption that all nomads are out to cheat him, a compromise figure of £200 for camel, food and passage was finally agreed to. The agreement was drawn up and witnessed by the Sous-Préfet. Considering that I had no idea what a kilo of rice cost, let alone a camel, I hoped that I had not been cheated too outrageously.

Just before we signed the agreement, the Sous-Préfet turned to me. 'Are you sure you want to go?' he said.

'Yes, I am sure.'

'The way will be very hard, and they will make no allowances for you.'

'I know, and I am sure.'

'Are you?' he said, and then he stopped. It was as if he was about to say something, then thought better of it.

'You will of course come to dine with me tonight,' he said, quickly covering the silence.

I accepted and left him. As I walked down the steps outside his office, into the heat of the middle of the day, I wondered just what it was that he had so 'almost' said to me.

He received me that evening, sipping lemonade by his swimming-pool. Like many practising Moslems he abstained from alcohol. Apart from the Persian carpet covered with rich designs, his dining-room was bare, a very Islamic room, stark and simple, like the Koran and the desert around.

It was not yet time for the evening meal, so we sat and talked. As so often happens when you meet educated exiles in raw, out-of-the-way places, we quickly exchanged life-stories. During the Algerian Revolution he had been a guerrilla with the F.L.N. in Ain-Sefra, the town where he was born. There he had become one of the leaders of the revolt. It was during the fighting that he met his wife. She was the first woman in southern Algeria to join the F.L.N., and now she worked in Bechar for the women's liberation movement in Algeria. Later he had to flee across the border into Morocco. After the cease-fire between the Algerians and the French, he was appointed a liaison officer with the French Army. The only reason why he had been given that job, he said, was because he wrote poetry. 'They imagined that I would be able to dance with the officers' wives.' He had started writing poetry as a young man in Paris. He had been writing it since. He was a lucky man, he told me, his wife did not object. 'Ours is a perfect marriage. I like writing poetry and my wife likes listening to it.'

He jumped up suddenly and offered to take me round his garden. He had something to show me. He led me down a succession of tidy paths, through a series of well-irrigated flower beds, past a clump of high palm trees to an enclosure at the end of the garden. There he introduced me to his prize possession, a pet gazelle that he had found when it was still young. Hunters had killed the mother, he said. The sleek and delicate animal shivered with fear as I came up to her and ran away. But when I withdrew she came right up to the Sous-Préfet, gently rubbing her face against his legs.

As we made our way back through the garden, I compared the Sous-Préfet to Prospero, with Tindouf as his island and the club-footed government clerk as a far-fetched Ariel.

'Oh no. Prospero was a magician. I am a mere civil servant.'
Then he sniggered slightly to himself and spoke with hands
gesturing.

'I am more like Napoleon with Tindouf as my St Helena . . . a
man in magnificent exile.' He clearly loved Tindouf.

'And Josephine alas is liberating the women of Bechar,' I
said, entering the spirit of the thing.

'And the others as well, alas.'

'But Napoleon must have many admirers in Tindouf?'

'Oh, he does. But if I so much as look at another woman here
she will imagine herself to be Miss World, and my authority does
not stretch that far.'

Then he told me that I was not the first English person that he
met at Tindouf. There had been two English girls before me.
They had appeared suddenly out of a lorry. They were on their
way through Africa, and stayed in Tindouf waiting for another
lorry to take them across the frontier into Mauritania. One of
them had dropped out of one of the redbrick universities. The
other was at some art school or other. He described them
minutely and lovingly. I could picture them heaving their rucksacks down the dusty streets as nonchalantly as if they were
walking down a side-street off the wrong end of the Portobello
Road. How those two girls managed to survive in Africa, their
honour intact, is a question that had continually haunted the
Sous-Préfet. I think that he was far more concerned about their
'honour' than they were. He urged them to abandon their
journey. Did they know the dangers that they were letting themselves in for? In Tindouf they were safe. They were under his
personal protection. But what would happen to them when they
crossed the frontier? He begged them to go home, but they would
not listen. A year later the Sous-Préfet got a letter from one of
them. They were safe and happy. One of them had a baby and the
other was going to get married. He told me this with a note of
sadness. He was a lonely man and I think that, in a very abstract
way, he was in love with both of them.

We ate our meal in silence. As we ate I studied the man. He
may have been lonely—who wouldn't be in his situation?—but
he was able to cope with his loneliness more easily than most of

us. For he had developed an acceptance of life and a peace of mind that spread around him, calming the most violent of temperaments.

After the meal we sat down by the floodlit swimming-pool, sipping lemonade in silence, like old friends who had no need to talk.

A poem from the T'ang Dynasty came to me, second-hand from an English novel. 'Here at the frontier there are fallen leaves. Although my neighbours are all barbarians, and you, you are a thousand miles away, there are always two cups at our table.'

'Do you like the bedouins?' I asked. I almost said 'barbarians'.

'Of course I do. There are a lot of them. And besides,' he added more seriously, using his hands to help him, 'we were all bedouins once.'

I complimented him on his surroundings: his house, his garden, his swimming-pool, and his gazelle.

Apart from the gazelle, he said, they were only there to impress the impressionable.

'Take a good look,' he said, smiling. 'This is what happens to revolutionaries who do not die when they are young. They end up like me.'

Yet he did his best to keep life simple. He had neither a secretary, nor a bodyguard, nor a chauffeur.

'I do not have a secretary because I do not think it right to have people doing the work that you ought to do yourself, and because it takes as long to explain what you want done as to do it yourself. I do not have a bodyguard because ... Well, you've heard the story of the Roman emperor who had no bodyguard, and when an assassin crept in, he saw the sleeping man and, thinking that he was the bodyguard, he crept by ... And I do not have a chauffeur because ... Let me explain: if I had an intelligent chauffeur, then I would have to talk to him, and if I had a stupid chauffeur ... Well, who wants a stupid chauffeur?'

All together I spent two weeks in Tindouf, sliding into the slow and sleepy oasis life with ease, basking in the apathy and irresponsibility that the sun imposed.

One day, feeling restless, I took a walk in the street. The sun was at its zenith. There was no one about. I closed my eyes to protect them from flying dust, and when I opened them again I saw a strange figure before me.

He looked more like an eagle than a human being. His long matted hair and his full black beard gave him the appearance of one who had come out of a child's nightmare. His face and body were smeared in oil. The few clothes he wore were tattered and smeared in oil and grease, which made him look as if he were clothed in black feathers. Yet though he wore rags, he wore them with distinction; unself-conscious and uncaring, as Caliban would have done.

I watched this rare specimen of humanity for some time. Later I asked the Sous-Préfet who he was.

'He is the Fool, the Holy Fool.'

'Does he always wear those clothes?'

'Oh, yes,' he said with a shrug. 'We've given him lots of nice ones, but he only tears them up.'

The next day, outside Tindouf's only café, I came upon the Holy Fool again. He stared and then started shouting in fury. Evidently he too had been asking questions.

'He is offended by the presence of a *nasrani* in the town,' the café owner casually translated into French as he washed the dishes.

The Holy Fool came closer. His eyes were severe, deeply sunk into his savage and determined face. They were frightening eyes, eyes that never winced, never deviated. I looked away, trying to pretend he wasn't there, like a Londoner confronted by a drunk in the Tube. But my attempts to ignore him only infuriated him the more. Then he started throwing stones.

What would you have done if you had had stones thrown at you in the same circumstances? After all, it would have been undignified to have thrown them back, yet it would have been even more undignified to have run away. You would probably have ended up doing exactly what I did: just stood there, looking stupid, until it was all over.

But the drama had not gone unobserved. Within a few minutes half the township had collected around in a semi-circle, and in the sea of faces I recognized a familiar figure in a crumpled white suit. As the Holy Fool came closer, I saw the crumpled white suit hop off to a nearby barracks. He came back with a detachment of military police. They took the Holy Fool away.

About half an hour later I saw him again. He was sitting cross-legged outside the office of the Sous-Préfet, with two military police on either side of him. The Sous-Préfet was standing on the steps with the government clerk a couple of steps below him. The Sous-Préfet was shaking his finger disapprovingly, but the Holy Fool was ignoring him. Unrepentant Caliban. He was just staring ahead of him, unaware of the crowd that had re-gathered to stare, unaware of the rebukes of Prospero. He was listening to something else; listening to it coldly, with neither emotion nor despair. What was it? Some strange god that had conquered his distraught mind? The 'demon of noontide' that Cassian wrote of? I didn't know. All I knew was that, whatever it was, it put him on a different level from the rest of us. Beside him even the Sous-Préfet was reduced to a banal little man.

That evening I apologized to the Sous-Préfet for the trouble that my presence as a *nasrani* had caused. I hoped that the Holy Fool was not going to be kept in prison on my account.

'Oh no. This happens regularly. Then he becomes a danger to everyone. If it had not been you it would have been someone else. In two days time there will be a "revolutionary festival" to celebrate the twenty-first anniversary of the Algerian Revolution. We cannot have him throwing stones at all those important people on the rostrum. That would be a terrible tragedy,' he said, with his tongue in his cheek.

Two days later, well after dusk, the entire population of Tindouf made their way to one of the Army forts outside the town for the opening of the Festival. The sexes divided as was customary and formed a semi-circle to the east of the fort. At midnight the Algerian flag was raised—green for fertility, white for Paradise and red for the blood that was shed—and twenty-one guns fired a salute, one gun for each year of the Revolution. With each artillery flash the whole sky lit up and then there was a brief silence until the boom of the gun could be heard over and over again as it echoed in the cliffs, or hammada, around. When the salute was finished three rockets shot up into the air, one green, one white and one red.

All that morning columns of Meharists had been coming into Tindouf. The Saharan Camelry Corps, or Meharists as they are called after their fast camels, was created in 1901 by a French Army Officer, Marie Joseph François Henri Laperrine. Like the Englishman, T. E. Lawrence, Laperrine did not try to fight the desert; instead he surrendered himself to it. He served in the Sahara for forty years, studying it, developing it and pacifying it. In the end he died in it, dying of thirst in a sandstorm. When they found his body there was still a little water left in his canteen; he had saved it for his companions.

Using nomad tribesmen in whom he placed absolute trust, Laperrine's Meharists brought law and order into the Sahara, something that the regular French Army had tried to do for fifty years and had spectacularly failed. They travelled light and fast, at an average speed of forty miles per day, twice the normal speed of a camel caravan The y defeated the Tuaregs, protected the Askia (the twice-yearly salt caravan from Taoudenni for Timbuktu), established a trans-Saharan postal service and even guarded the Allies' southern flank during the North African campaigns in the 1939–45 War. After Independence the French handed them over to the Algerians. They still patrol the desert frontier, a cross between policemen and lifeboatmen that the Land-Rover is unable to surpass.

The next day they poured through Tindouf, swinging their magnificent battle-camels through the streets in full-tribal dress. Their camels were enormous, and the bright blankets that covered their saddles gave them a fleeting colourful appearance. The male onlookers who thronged the streets cheered, and the blue and black lines of bedouin women 'lu-laied' them as they roared past.

They came in waves. The clouds of dust that swirled around their camels' legs played tricks on the eyes so that they looked as if they were floating on some heavy gas. Above their flowing turbans and gleaming rifles their banners skipped in the wind. The noise of the camels' hooves was deafening. Neither Attila's cavalry galloping westwards, nor Giap's tribal irregulars massed in the mountains above Dien Bien Phu, could have looked more magnificent.

The Festival was over, and the Sous-Préfet told me that I

would soon be leaving Tindouf for Tahar Omar's encampment. My feelings were mixed. I was anxious to get started, but I was also fearful for the future. 'Hell-hole of a place' . . . 'not fit for human habitation' . . . 'even under the most merciless regimes'. The descriptions of Taoudenni went round and round my mind like an Irish jig, getting nowhere.

And there were other fears too. Helen Waddell's *Lives of the Fathers* had added a new dimension to my journey, a dimension 'beyond sound of voice or movement of the tongue', and it frightened me. One day I climbed up the Hammada of Tindouf to look out over the desert that I was about to enter. As I looked out over the ominous, dry and lifeless expanse of the Iguidi Desert, a fragment from Islamic mysticism came to me.

'They tell me that you possess the pearl of divine knowledge: either give it to me or sell it to me.'

'I cannot sell it because you do not have the price for it, and I cannot give it because then you would have gained it too cheaply.'

'Then what do I do?'

'Cast yourself headlong, like me, into this ocean in order that you may win the pearl by waiting patiently.'

'Cast yourself headlong . . .' I thought of the Holy Fool and I shuddered.

I saw the Holy Fool one last time. It was the evening before my departure. His fit had passed and he had been released from prison. The time was dusk; it was the hour of prayer. I could hear the muezzin in his tower above the mosque singing out the words of the Azan. 'I bear witness that there is none worthy of worship save Allah. I bear witness that Mohammed is the messenger of Allah.' The Holy Fool was standing alone on the Hammada, silhouetted against the dying day, defying the winds, the fretful elements, even God himself. He stood straight against the sky with his arms stretched out above him, calling out to his god with great force, shouting to some being that he, and only he, was aware of. He was not praying as other Moslems pray, in awe of his god, bowing and kneeling in servitude. He prayed as an equal, standing up proudly and confidently. He had found his god and was speaking to him, while I, a mere mortal, could only stare in

wonder. And as I watched him pray and listened to the blasts of
the wind, I could almost hear his god reply.

That night I dined with the Sous-Préfet for the last time. After
we had eaten the couscous I complimented him on the Arab's
legendary hospitality.

He smiled.

'Have you heard the story of the Arab stallion from Seville?'
he asked.

'No, I haven't.'

'During the reign of Queen Isabella an Arab lived in Seville.
There was war between the Arabs and the Christians, but Seville
had been conquered by the Christians some time before, so no
one bothered this harmless old Arab who lived there with his
wife and a most beautiful stallion. The beauty and the fame of
that stallion spread all over Spain, so one day a courtier of Queen
Isabella's, hearing of this stallion, decided he would try to buy it
to give to the Queen as a present. He came to the house of the
old Arab and knocked on the door. "Before we discuss any
business," said the Arab, "you must first sample our great Moslem
hospitality." "But we have nothing in the house," the Arab's wife
whispered to the old man. "Oh yes we have," the man told his
wife. "Go and prepare." The courtier sat down, the Arab still
refusing to discuss the business that had brought the courtier to
him. A great dish of meat was brought in . . .' His voice trailed
away. There was no point in continuing.

'And now you must sample Tindouf's hospitality,' he said
and clapped his hands.

A great dish of meat was brought in.

'Camel meat,' said the Sous-Préfet.

We ate the meal in silence. I wondered what it all meant. The
evening wore on and after several hours it was time to go. I
thanked him for everything that he had done to help me.

'One last word of advice. Do everything that they do, and do
not express your surprise at anything.'

I looked at him, and on his face I could detect a shadow of a
smile. What was it for? What did it mean? It was the smile of
some knowledgeable person, someone who understood something that I did not understand, who knew something that I did

not know. Then he took in a breath, as if he wanted to say something, and for the second time since I had met him I felt that he was holding out on something that he thought better not to tell me.

'What was it you were going to say?'

'It is nothing.'

I left him and packed my baggage. It did not take long; I had very little to pack. Then I lay on my bed waiting for the lorry that Tahar Omar had rented to take his merchandise to the encampment at Chegga. Four o'clock, it was not there. Five o'clock, it still had not arrived. Then, a little before six, it roared up, gave two hoots on its horn and braked to a halt. I jumped up, ran outside, threw my baggage in the back, and climbed onto the lorry. It ground into gear and I fell over amidst a confusion of sacks and boxes. We were off into the uncertainty.

For that was how I left for the frontier. Uncertain of the future, uncertain of myself, and uncertain of that shadow of a smile.

3

A Walk on the Wild Side

The way ahead was sombre. The flat landscape of sand and stones seemed to stretch to the very ends of the earth. Above our heads the sun glared down without pity, its white light blinding what faded colours there were; around the sun the two buzzards dived and circled, playing games with the force of gravity.

There was nothing orderly about Tahar Omar's caravan. Some of us walked and others rode. Men shouted and camels roared. It was hardly the 'off' that I had expected. At its constant pace of two and a half miles an hour, the walking pace of a man and a camel, our caravan looked tiny and pathetic stretched out across the desert floor in its irregular and haphazard fashion.

We drifted on for several hours within vague limits half-heartedly imposed by the Half-Child at the front, Dermas the slave at the back, and the two blue-robed outriders prancing like fussy butterflies on either flank. At midday Omar beckoned me forward. I beat my camel into a disjointed trot and rode up to him.

'Today we will march thirty kilometres,' he said, looking down on me from his big white bull. (Omar was always looking down at me.) 'Tomorrow we will march thirty-five and the next day forty. Then, *Inshallah*, we shall be at the well of Bouir Ikrief, where we will drink water for the last time. After it will be all speed to Taoudenni, more than twelve days away.'

I remembered the words of the Sous-Préfet. 'Do as they do and do not express your surprise at anything.' I tried to look nonchalant and at ease.

'I hope that the slow pace at the beginning is not for my benefit?' I said to Omar.

'Of course not,' he replied, astonished that I should even mention such an idea. 'It is not for your benefit, *Nasrani*. It is for the camels'.'

We never travelled thirty kilometres that day, nor thirty-five the next. Omar never kept his word on distances—or anything else for that matter which could be delegated to the authority of *Inshallah*. An hour after he had given me his provisional time-table, he motioned the caravan to halt. I looked up at him questioningly.

'Over there,' he said, pointing to a few slender shoots of grass. 'There is grazing. Only God knows if there is any further on.'

I will always remember that first day out. It was new and brightly-painted, like the shining red fire-engine of my earliest recollection. Time has not dulled it, nor has routine blunted it, and besides, I was giddy with the novelty of everything around me. I had left behind me the common regions of universal experience, and was walking across the desert towards 'a bit of one's own', to use Conrad's phrase. From now on every move, every decision, every gamble, indeed every step that took me nearer Taoudenni would be a very personal triumph.

I now realize that that day was a deceptive one. The endless hours of boredom, weariness and dissatisfaction were yet to come. Yet that day remains dominant in my memory. It established a rhythm to the ones that followed and gave my life a pattern—and thus, a sense of security—that I was to conform to, almost without exception, until I reached the salt-mines of Taoudenni.

The days began with prayers.

'Come to prayer, come to prayer,' Omar barked out amid a background chorus of coughs and hacks. 'Come to success, come to success. Prayer is better than sleep.' He spoke to his god in a no-nonsense manner, with the same tone of voice that he would use with any other creditor.

After Omar had called out to pray, the nomads would gather together to wash before prayer, using sand, instead of water, to cleanse themselves. After they had lined up facing the east and prayed, they gathered round the feeble beginnings of a fire, huddling together to warm themselves from the early morning cold. They sat on their haunches slowly and laboriously talking. Each time a nomad came up, the men round the fire would rise onto their feet to greet him. '*Salam alaikum.*' '*Alaikum wa salam.*' How beautiful those salutations sounded.

Dunes in the Erg Cherch Desert

Loading a camel

Saddling a camel

While Omar made early morning tea, Dermas would be cooking a spicy porridge that had been built up with the scraps from the previous night's meal. Although the hot porridge burnt the throat, it warmed the body and filled the stomach, helping me to face the journey ahead.

After breakfast the camels would be rounded up and brought into camp to be saddled and loaded. Rounding up the hobbled camels could take anything from five minutes to two hours. In spite of the tight ropes that the nomads twist around their forelegs like handcuffs, hobbled camels can hop incredible distances. In one night a camel may hop ten miles in his search for grazing. But that, fortunately, is rare.

With the exception of Omar's white bull, all the camels in the caravan were small and in poor condition. But I noticed, with a certain sinking feeling, that my camel was in the worst condition of all.

There had been a long drought in the Sahara, Omar reminded me. Except for an occasional very light shower, there had been no rain in the desert for seven years. Omar's camels, like all other desert creatures, were weak from hunger and fatigue.

The camels of the Sahara are single-humped. Unlike in Arabia where the females are ridden, only the males are used in the Sahara. Female camels, like female nomads, are kept in the encampment for milking and child-rearing.

When the camels had been brought in, the business of saddling and loading would begin. With a jerk of the headrope and a slow hissing sound from between the teeth, the nomads would couch the camels. There was no sympathy for objectors. Troublesome camels would have their nostrils grabbed by a hooked forefinger and be hauled down by their nose.

A camel's descent from a standing to a kneeling position is a long and complicated affair. They flop down onto their forelegs, settle onto their hindknees, then sink onto their hocks. Once they are on the ground, they are tightly hobbled with ropes twisted round their doubled-up forelegs. Particularly aggressive camels would have a rope slung across them from one foreleg to the other, pinioning down their necks. Camels regularly try to attack their loaders. Later I was to meet a man who lost half his right foot in a fight with a camel.

E

Saddling and loading were always noisy and chaotic. The camels would roar and snarl when approached, belching half-regurgitated curd out of their mouths. A camel's roar carries for miles across the desert. I once asked Omar how bedouins used to keep their camels silent in the days of tribal raids, when surprise was so essential. He picked up a twisted piece of rope that had been used to hobble a camel and twisted it round my face, closing my mouth.

The actual saddling of a camel is relatively simple. A blanket is thrown across the camel's hump, and either a riding saddle or a pack saddle is slung on top of it. The saddle that Omar had sold me, for the ridiculously large sum of ten pounds, was a Mauritanian saddle. If it had not been for the dangerously large pommel in the front, it would have looked something like an armchair with wings on it. It was made out of a wooden structure with leather stretched over it, which made a hollow in the centre, which was easy to sit upon.

'It is extremely hard to fall out of,' Omar told me encouragingly when he sold it to me. 'Perfect for a beginner.'

The Mauritanian saddle is much heavier than the flimsy Malian saddle that I was to see further south. The Malian saddle is made of three pieces of wood, with a pommel and backrest. It is very hard to ride on. As well as being comfortable, the Mauritanian saddle has another great advantage. Its two wings act as sunshades, and when the sun is at its highest, it is often possible to walk along close by your camel in the shade.

Another blanket or sheepskin rug would then be thrown on top, and a noose tightened around the saddle's 'neck'. From this we hung our entire portable world: waterskins, saddlebags, food, clothes, and cooking utensils.

The importance of correct loading cannot be over-estimated; a badly balanced load is a threat to the entire caravan, Omar told me, in his easy, patronizing way. If the load slipped the camel might panic; this might spread among the other camels and soon the entire caravan would bolt. Elaborate precautions were taken to ensure that a camel's load was evenly distributed, and on our first few days out we were constantly stopping to shift loads. The art of loading a camel is to spread and balance, making sure that there are no hard edges rubbing against the camel's sides. Omar told me that a well-loaded camel should be able to move at ease, without a girth and with a man on top, without it over-balancing.

When the loading was finished, the six goatskins that we kept our water in were distributed amongst the three strongest camels. The skins were strung on either side of the camel's hump. The outsides of the skins looked vile and dirty, covered in hair and sand, wet with the camel pee that the animals sprayed around themselves generously. Yet inside they were clean and cured. The neck and the legs had been cut off, and the legs and the anus sewn up to prevent the water splashing out. The neck, or spout, was tied together with cord and the four legs were attached to ropes that hung down from the camel's hump.

Every night Omar carefully checked these skins for leaks, treating them with rancid butter to keep the leather in good condition. Yet in spite of his care, two of them leaked profusely. The first time that I saw them I was struck with horror at the thought of our lives depending on these primitive water-holders. Now I take back that first impression. Canvas water-bags would leak, plastic ones would melt in the heat, and steel or tin ones would rub sores on the camels' flanks. No modern invention can beat the goatskin as a safe and efficient carrier of water for the desert nomad.

Saddled and loaded, the camels were ready for mounting. Mounting a camel I found was far harder than actually riding one. Standing on the left side of the camel, facing forwards, you swing your right leg over the pommel, grab it with both hands and somehow perform a sideways vault. It is a dangerous business. Before you have begun to find your balance, the camel will have started to rise. First the camel raises its hindlegs and comes up onto its knees. This pushes you forward onto its neck. Next it raises its forelegs with the same series of motions. This throws you backwards. Then it brings its hindlegs up to a standing position. This sends you flying forward again, and after that it comes up on its forelegs, throwing you backwards.

With the high pommel in front of the saddle, there is a very grave risk involved in mounting. Several times I misjudged my timing and, feeling a shot of pain between my legs, feared a fate almost as bad as death.

With the exception of Omar, all the nomads could mount with ease. Poor Omar. Right up until we got to Taoudenni he had to ask Dermas to act as a mounting-block. Once mounted, however, Omar was a different man. On his camel he was supreme and all-powerful. With an utterance to God and a movement of his wrist his orders went unchallenged. None save a god, or the captain of a ship, know such power.

Few of the nomads bothered with saddles. They were quite happy perched on their camels' humps, sitting on blankets. Sometimes they sat on their haunches, sometimes cross-legged, sometimes with their legs astride. Sitting on my Mauritanian saddle I felt at a disadvantage. While it may have been hard to fall out of, it was very restricting, and I envied the other nomads the ease with which they could move around.

Only the Half-Child, who led the caravan towing Omar's white bull, did not have a camel to ride. Nor did he have shoes for that matter. As the youngest in the caravan he was the most insignificant. On Omar's ladder, just as there had to be someone at the top, so there had to be someone at the bottom, without camel and without shoes.

Occasionally, during a particularly long march, Omar would allow the Half-Child to sit in front of him on the white bull's neck. Sitting there on the camel, Omar and the black boy would chat away as the mood took them. Don't get me wrong. Omar was not patronizing. Like so many other illiterate people he was able to talk to a child as an equal. I think it was this that made me put total trust in Tahar Omar. This ability to talk to children as equals is not, of course, dependent on illiteracy. But it is dependent on goodness. The quality of amusing and interesting children, Claud Cockburn wrote in his autobiography, 'is a sign of goodness. Many good men cannot do it very well. But no bad man can do it at all.'[1] Tahar Omar was a good man.

In spite of the horror stories that I had heard in England about camel-riding, I found that the actual riding was simple and straightforward—a typical amateur's over-confidence. If I wanted

[1] Claud Cockburn, *I, Claud . . .*, Harmondsworth, 1967.

to go right, I would tap the camel with my riding-stick on the right side of his neck. If I wanted to go left, then I would tap him on the left. If I wanted to stop him or slow him down, I would just give a gentle tug on the headrope, and if I wanted to lower him to a couch, then I just hissed. The only problem was to go faster. My camel, whom I named *Mr Wilson,* was loath to go any faster than he had to, and it took the hardest of wallops on his behind to get him to break into a funeral march. Altogether I was astonished at the ease with which I learnt to ride a camel. Each time I learnt something new, the nomads smiled encouragingly. Only Omar offered me no encouragement; he looked at my efforts at camel-riding with the same ill-disguised disgust with which he looked at my table manners.

A camel does not walk like a dog or a horse, with its four legs moving alternately. Instead it walks with the foreleg on one side followed by the hindleg on the same side, then the foreleg on the other side followed by the hindleg on that side. The result is an easy, swaying movement that swings your whole body from side to side, forcing you to surrender into its drunken, rolling gait.

I found walking to be much easier than trotting, which shook every bone in my body. This surprised me; most Europeans who have ridden camels have enthused about the joy of trotting but have had little good to say about walking. My father recalled reading the poems of Rupert Brooke on a trotting camel. Possibly it was because of the very sore bum that I quickly developed? I do not know. But I could not bear trotting. Galloping, I will admit, was great fun. It was cool, refreshing, and exhilarating. But I rarely got that chance. The caravan went no faster than walking pace, and Omar discouraged anything faster that might tire out the camels.

The camel is an ecological miracle. Unlike their cousins in the eastern Sahara who are grain-fed, these camels had no food supply save what they could grab from the land around. With sufficient grazing they can travel for fifteen days in between waterings; without grazing they are lucky to last five. The camel's rate of water elimination is one-third that of the average mammal, including the human being. Not only can he lose in liquid up to a quarter of his total weight without serious risk, but drinking at an average rate of two and a half gallons of water per minute, he can absorb that loss in a single watering.

The arrival of the camel in the Sahara did more to shape the economy and the society of the desert than any other single event, until the arrival of the motor car. Prior to the introduction of the camel into the Sahara, the desert was inhabited by a black race, troglodytes according to Herodotus, who were swift on foot and 'eat snakes and lizards and other reptiles and speak a language like nothing on earth—it could be bats screeching'.[2]

Like the inhabitants of the Kalahari Desert today, they were bushmen. These primitive men and women left their marks on the caves that they lived in, turning their underground homes into great art galleries full of rock paintings that gave a golden portrait of the light of early day. Naked and unalienated, they painted themselves as they hunted and they painted the animals that they hunted. Their testament has been found on rocks all over the Sahara.

Archaeologists have identified five different styles in these paintings, styles that bear a remarkable resemblance to similar ones found in France, Spain, and the Kalahari Desert. Each style seems to represent a stage in primitive man's evolution. In the earliest stage man is a small creature. He is dominated by the animals around him: the elephant, the rhino, the buffalo, and its now extinct predecessor, the Bubalus Antiquus. In the second stage man has grown in stature, and he is seen hunting the animals that had previously dominated him. In the third stage domestic animals make their appearance. There are cattle and dogs. Chariots can be seen pulled by horses, but so far the horse has not been ridden. In the fourth stage man is seen on horseback. It is not until the fifth and last stage, artistically the crudest of all, that the camel makes its appearance.

The arrival of the camel opened up new routes and new water-holes to man, bringing him into contact with the most isolated quarters of the desert. With the camel came hordes of Zenata Berbers, who swept across the Sahara, pushing the black races to the south, 'like a hoard of locusts', according to one chronicler. A few generations later the Arabs came, repeating the movement

[2] Herodotus, *The History, IV.*

that pushed the black races to the south, a historic movement still in motion today.

'With these changes,' wrote E. W. Bovill, 'came a new man to Africa, the camel-owning nomad, turbulent, predatory, elusive, and unassailable. Thus was civilization faced with a menace from which it has never since been wholly free and one which the legionaries of Rome never knew.'[3]

Yet sitting on my camel I felt neither turbulent, predatory, elusive, nor unassailable. My camel, I noticed as I fell further and further behind, was going far slower than the others. When I was walking I could drag him along at the same speed as the others, but the minute I got on top of him he came to a stop.

There are two types of camel in the Sahara I recalled, as I seethed with frustration, the camel or dromedary, and the baggage camel, the everyday beast of burden. The dromedary is lightly-coloured and finely-boned, capable of averaging forty miles in a day. Graceful and imposing, he is good at short fast sprints, but lacks endurance over long distances. He is less thickly furred, more delicately built, and better tempered than his proletarian cousin, the camel of the caravan routes. Although the baggage camel is smaller, he is sturdier and can carry weights of up to five hundred pounds with ease. The dromedary will collapse suddenly and die on the trail; the baggage camel will walk out his life on the caravan routes like some old soldier, until he finally fades away while pulling up water from some dark and depressing well.

Suddenly it occurred to me, as suddenly as St Paul's conversion on the road to Damascus, that I had been conned. Omar told me that the camel that I was going to buy, for a hundred and twenty of the two hundred pounds, was going to be a dromedary. But it was plain, even to a beginner like me, that *Mr Wilson*, as I called my camel, was a straight working-class baggage camel. He was no problem walking along beside me, of course he wasn't. He was used to that. What he was not used to was being ridden. He would tolerate me on his back, but he would only do it with a go-slow protest. No wonder he was so easy to ride. A cart-horse is easy to ride for someone who has never been on a horse.

I looked at Omar with smouldering resentment. He stared

[3] Bovill, *op. cit.*

back at me like a second-hand car salesman. But I couldn't keep
my resentment up. He might have outwitted me and made a
handsome profit out of it, but there was nothing malicious in
him. Omar was a sharp businessman, and he would have expected
me to play the same trick on him if I could. Besides, I recalled
with resignation, I was a *nasrani,* and that made me fair game for
such tricks. In Omar's eyes he was doing nothing but assist in
re-distributing the wealth of the world. He treated money as we
treat love and war. All was fair.

As I thought of the consequences of *Mr Wilson*'s resistance to
having me on his back, a sick feeling came over me. I realized
that if I was to keep up with the others and get to Taoudenni,
then I would have to walk most of the way there, pulling *Mr
Wilson* behind me.

We drifted on, our lives governed by the scarcity of grazing
and the will of God. As we moved across the dry and empty
land we gave our camels as much freedom as possible to stretch
out their long necks and grab what shoots of grass they could as
they meandered along. At times there would be a moment of
excitement when I saw an old broken calabash or some other
relic of man. For the country that we were travelling through
was one of the original homes of pre-cameline man. Huge primitive axes of Palaeolithic age have been found in the Erg Cherch.

It was during these long and monotonous hours that I began
to get to know my travelling companions. They were an extraordinary combination of opposites. At one moment proud,
arrogant and frank, at the next, grovelling, ingratiating and
dishonest. They would think nothing of walking twenty miles to
pass the time of day, but they would whimper and complain if
they had to walk twenty yards before they had had their morning
tea. They were unbelievable hypochondriacs, who lived in fear
of the slightest pain, yet they would think nothing of dying for
a single gesture. It was strange and disquieting to live among
people who would cheat you of everything you had, yet would
leap to your defence if you were attacked by strangers.

Their values were not those of a Westerner. They saw nothing
degrading in either poverty or begging, yet they regarded
meanness of pocket and meanness of spirit as the greatest of all

vices. They would treat their camels far better than they ever treated their women, but they had within them reserves of love and chivalry that would have put Chaucer's Knight to shame.

In spite of these virtues, however, I found the constant cadging and curiosity overwhelming.

'What is this?'

'It is . . .'

'What is it for?'

'It is for . . .'

'Give it to me.'

'No I need it.'

'But you are a *nasrani,* you are rich. I am poor, I have nothing.'

'Let me use it as well as you then.'

It was tiresome. Every answer resulted in a loss of face.

'And what is this?'

'May I use it too?'

'No, because only one person may use this.'

'Then let me use it. You are rich and I am poor.'

'No, you may not use it.'

'Why?'

Only Omar at the top of the social ladder and Dermas close to the bottom would not intervene in these exchanges. They left it to the *nasrani* to learn the hard way. Neither did either of them ask for anything that was not theirs. Dermas was too busy with the menial tasks of cameleering to be able to participate, and Omar clearly considered himself to be above all that. While the others were going through my belongings, asking about everything and demanding it all for themselves, Omar was greasing the water-skins, checking his goods, or simply intoning to himself verses from the Koran. Yet nothing escaped his tight, narrow little eyes. He saw everything and forgot nothing.

It was hard. The physical strain weakened my resistance and made the mental strain harder to bear. I felt isolated and self-conscious. I suspected the nomads of laughing at me. There was nothing new in this feeling. It has been felt by imperialists, missionaries, explorers, traders, and just plain vagabonds like myself. Didn't George Orwell say that the greatest fear of the Englishman in the East is the fear of being laughed at?

The blame for these moments of paranoia should fall on me. This was their country and their life-style. It was for me, not them, to make the compromises. As the name which they gave me, *el Nasrani*, made clear, I was nothing but an unclean stranger. And when I did try to change to their nomadic ways, I was applauded with enthusiasm and encouragement. Soon I changed from despising my fellow travellers to respecting them, from respecting them to admiring them, and from admiring them to loving them. I had come to the Sahara to find slaves. I found far more besides.

Sometimes we would travel for fourteen hours without stopping; at other times we would halt after only a couple of hours on the move. It all depended on the grazing. At first, because I insisted on seeing my journey in terms of an airport timetable, I found these continual delays infuriating. After a while, however, I just drifted along like everyone else, totally surrendering to the will of God, young and irresponsible in the freedom and the necessity of it all.

But it took time to reach that level of acceptance and resignation. At first my whole journey seemed punctuated by delays. There were times when I feared we would never reach Bouir Ikrief, let alone Taoudenni; and Timbuktu seemed several fantasies away. Like most Westerners, I had been taught to chop Time up into pieces, and after twenty-five years of urban life I found it hard to accept the fact that Time, as a definite and measured period, had stopped at Tindouf. So I clung on to the idea of it, frightened of what would happen to me if I let it go. I had come from a society that measured Time in terms of minutes, into a society that was not happy measuring it in terms of days. Time was no more. The past was dead, the future was in the hands of God, there was only the present. I thought of Stanley on his death-bed, listening to the chimes of Big Ben. 'So that, that is Time,' he said.

After we had unloaded and hobbled the camels, Dermas would dismiss them with a silent flick of his wrist, and they would shuffle off to find what grazing they could on that mean and barren land. With the camels taken care of, we would build a wind-break with the baggage and collect up dried roots to make a fire. I became quite good at picking out the tiny stems that protruded from the ground with an enormous cluster of thick roots underneath them spreading out under the sand to suck in every drop of moisture around.

Caillié had seen the same foliage a hundred and fifty years earlier on his journey back to Europe from Timbuktu:

These plants have short and flexible leaves; the thorn is short but very hard; by the wise providence of Nature this plant, the only resource of the animals of the desert, has the property of remaining green all the year round, in spite of the burning east winds which so frequently prevail; the camels though not very delicate would refuse the dry leaves. This plant is very tenacious of life, throws out long roots on the surface of the ground, and does not grow to a height of more than eighteen inches; it is found in sandy places, and I have generally observed that it is more abundant on the west side of hills. The roots are thick and serve for fuel; the Moors use it to cook their provisions, and at sun-set the slaves went to collect it, to boil our scanty portion of rice with water and salt, to which they added melted butter for sauce; this was our frugal supper. [4]

When the firewood had been collected and the fire had been lit, we would sit on our haunches waiting for tea, while a scroll of smoke slowly rose into the sky. When tea had finally been served, the sitting-around, tea-drinking, eating and talking began. It took us far into the night.

Usually I tried to join in these evening conversations, but after an hour of heavy mental strain I usually gave up. Although nomads are one of the most individualistic races in the world, they have absolutely no understanding of privacy. Sometimes I found the loneliness of living among alien people so crushing that I would take myself off into the desert alone, just to be by myself. But my companions were offended by this anti-social behaviour, and remembering the advice of the Sous-Préfet to 'do as they do', I forced myself to give this pleasure up. After that, my sleeping-bag was the only escape that I had. I would lie in it, looking up at the stars, while the night became clear and lucid.

[4] Caillié, *op. cit.*, Vol. II.

There I would hover for a while, in the blurred regions between sleep and wakefulness, until finally I faded into another world.

The nomads camped, ate and slept in the closest proximity to each other. It was as if my companions wanted to escape from the vast empty spaces all around by drawing into themselves, so close that it was claustrophobic. Yet in spite of the total absence of women, I never encountered one case of homosexuality among these Arabs, even though they did sleep next to each other for protection from the cold. They did not even masturbate. I think that the extremes of heat and cold made everyone totally sexless.

When I awoke on my second morning, the call of the muezzin was the only sound in the world. I tried to get up but felt so stiff I could hardly move. Thanks to his radio, Omar had heard that the English drank tea. Was *nasrani* tea different from Arab tea, he asked. I told him it was. I had brought some Indian tea with me, so I offered Omar a sample of black Indian tea, mixed with sugar and condensed milk. There is little to say about that cultural exchange except that from then on Omar regarded *nasrani* tea as a punishment inflicted on disbelievers by Allah, the exact reason for which God, in his infinite wisdom, would reveal at a later date—no doubt.

We travelled that day over the same blank landscape. It was empty and infinite, unfamiliar and featureless. We shrank beside the enormity of it all. The ever-blowing north-east wind had blown all the fine sand off the plain, or *reg* as the Arabs call it, leaving behind a bare surface of stones and gravel. It was to be this type of *reg* that was to be the dominant feature of the desert between Tindouf and Timbuktu.

About midday the *reg* was interrupted by chaotic heaps of tumbled-down boulders. Stony valleys slashed and disfigured the *reg*'s flat surface. We hopped and danced across the haphazard confusion for about a mile, and then we found ourselves back on the same monotonous *reg* that we had been travelling on all morning. Above us the sun beat down, blinding our eyes. Below us its reflection rebounded off the shining stones of the *reg*. I tried to look ahead, but the flat horizon was vague and broken up, shimmering in the heat like an airport runway in June.

There was less talking on that second day out of Chegga. The heat and the beginnings of boredom dulled the brain. During that entire day I was only asked a question once. 'Mood, shouting from one of the flanks and waving his rifle in the air to attract my attention, asked me what it was that I missed most. Was it women? I already suspected them of laughing at me and I was determined not to give them any more ammunition, so I told them—which was true—that women were the last thing on my mind. What I missed most was tobacco. 'Mood shouted back that with God's will I should have tobacco. I thought no more of it and walked on through the Saharan day in silence.

About four o'clock there was chaos. My saddle-bag got loose and slipped off *Mr Wilson*'s back, getting tangled up in his feet. *Mr Wilson* reared up, broke free of the headrope I was holding, and galloped off, dragging a trail of my belongings behind him. A flood of Omarian abuse was hurled at me. He shouted at me to study the way a camel was loaded more carefully. I was not only a hindrance, he went on, I was a danger. Dermas, without a word, had caught the camel and was bringing it back. Omar shouted at him not to do the *nasrani*'s work for him, and then the whole caravan stopped while I collected up my belongings.

Sometime that day we crossed the frontier into Mali. The landscape looked no different, there were no sudden changes. I would not even have known that we had crossed the frontier if Omar had not told me. 'Another frontier crossed,' I wrote in my journal. 'Theoretically my seven-day visa for Bamako starts today!'

That night we camped in Mali. I expected to dream of the frontier, but I dreamt of pillarboxes and Trollope instead.

We did not leave the following morning, our first morning in Mali. According to Omar, more camels were needed to take his merchandise to Taoudenni. Without more camels we would have to turn round and head back to Chegga. So Dermas and el Kiad were dispatched to the south, Mohammed to the west, 'Mood and Kahil to the east, and Lehia went north; all looking for nomad encampments where they might buy camels.

Omar, the Half-Child and myself stayed behind. Omar sent the Half-Child off to watch the grazing camels and then set about the business of the day. He checked the waterskins, baked bread, and made yet another inventory of his goods. He was like a well run family firm. If Omar was an aristocrat, as the Sous-Préfet had told me, a lord of the desert, then he was a very hard-working one. He threw himself into his tasks with dedication and a sense of industry. The Protestant ethic was deeply ingrained in his unquestioning Moslem beliefs.

Occasionally he would stop his work and let his eyes wander over the empty spaces, scanning the nothingness around him like a guru, or a man whittling. Then, suddenly, he would catch himself doing it and return to the task in hand, annoyed at his own lack of concentration. With two wives, two houses and a radio to support, he could not afford leisure.

At midday he called the Half-Child back and made tea. Sitting there under the inadequate shade of a crippled tree, brewing tea, there was something very benevolent about him. After tea he turned on his radio. There was news of the Spanish Saharan situation. Morocco was making fresh claims on the territory and Spain had announced that they would resist. Omar spent some of his time in 'Spain', as he called the Spanish Sahara, and he feared that fighting would be bad for business. I asked him his opinions on the Moroccan claims. He spat on a patch of sand.

'No one troubles us in "Spain". There are no police asking questions, nor are we expected to pay any taxes. The Spanish stay in the towns. "Spain" is the only country left where you can buy and sell slaves without being troubled. They don't want to be liberated from "colonial oppression".'

For the first and last time on my journey I got Omar to talk a little of politics. His politics were those of any other sensible small businessman. He went with the tide.

'When I am in Mali I am a capitalist. I like money and business and I listen to the "Voice of America" on the radio. When I am in Algeria I am a socialist, because the Algerians give away *dowa* (medicine) and I can have my teeth taken out when they hurt. But when I am in Morocco I am not a Moroccan, because I have my dignity. But when I am in "Spain", he said with a grin, "I am a nomad because no one bothers me there.'

Omar's economic opinions were interesting too. He told me

that Algeria was better to live in than Morocco, but Mali was
better for business. The Algerian police and government were
honest, he told me, while the Moroccans were only out for
themselves. But in Algeria he had to pay higher taxes and so, at
tax time, he preferred to do business in Mali from his Timbuktu
house and then return to Algeria in the summer. Tahar Omar
was more than just a caravan-master. He was an international
tax-dodger.

As far as the Spanish Sahara went—the main topic of conversation in the nomad encampments—Omar was not optimistic. He
had a deep-seated dislike of the Moroccan government and he
feared a take-over. The tribes in the south of 'Spain', he said,
would resist them. There was talk of war, and of a new force that
would resist the Moroccans. (I now know that he was referring
to the left-wing Polisario Front, the Front for the Liberation of
Sekia el Hama and Rio de Oro.) The Rguibat would probably
fight against Morocco. But for the Tradjakant it was more
serious. There were Tradjakants in Morocco who supported the
Moroccan demand. Others in Algeria and Mauritania opposed it.
There was a danger of the entire tribe splitting over the Spanish
Sahara and fighting a civil war. War was bad, he said, trade would
suffer. Already the caravans had stopped coming down from
Morocco.

Then all of a sudden he clamped up.

'Why do you want to know, *Nasrani*?'

'What concern is it of yours?'

'Why is it that you always ask questions?'

He looked at me with scorn and then lapsed into a sulk. A man
with a wife and a house in Mali, a wife and a house in Algeria,
business connections in 'Spain', and a hearty dislike of Morocco,
cannot be too careful when he talks politics to strangers.

I wandered away, leaving him alone in his silence. I felt
alienated and distant and could have done with a cigarette. As I
lurked around the camp, feeling bored and useless, I came upon
a deep green plant, a North African variety of the loco-weed. I
bent down to examine it.

'Do not eat that, *Nasrani*,' Omar shouted. 'It will make you
weak in the head.'

Remembering the Sous-Préfet's advice, I didn't eat it. I tried smoking it, but it didn't work.

Lehia, 'Mood and Kahil returned that afternoon. Lehia had found nothing, but 'Mood and Kahil, following fresh tracks, had come across a nomad encampment about half a day away. There were no camels for sale, 'Mood said, but the encampment did have something. Then he turned to me and produced from under his robes a thin, silver-stemmed, nomad pipe and an old leather pouch full of tobacco.

'For you, *Nasrani*,' 'Mood said. 'You said yesterday that you missed tobacco.'

I was suspicious at first. I feared that there was an ulterior motive behind the gift. How wrong I was; how ashamed I am now for thinking it.

The next morning Mohammed, who had come back during the night, spotted two outlines on the horizon, moving in our direction. I could hardly see them.

'It is two camels,' he said with confidence. 'From their size they are mother and child.'

We waited a long time in silence, while they slowly meandered towards us. After an hour they were within sprinting distance, walking towards our own hobbled camels. In a split second the nomads were on their feet and rushing at the camels with their long graceful strides. The camels turned in terror. Too late, they were surrounded.

They galloped off in panic, trying to break out of the ever-decreasing circle, but wherever they ran they were headed off by humans. Suddenly they stopped in their tracks, frozen in fear. Ignoring the young one, the nomads went for the mother. Two of them grabbed her long spindly legs, two others took the neck. The Half-Child grabbed the tail. Omar, who had waddled up as fast as he could, just leaned. The she-camel crashed to the ground.

With her head pinioned down, she kicked in desperation. While a rope was being tightened around her forelegs, she fought back with a passion that seemed almost sexual. Sitting on her neck I felt her twist and lurch around in some masochistic orgasm. The hobbling operation completed, I looked around. Now I realized why she had twisted and lurched in such a fashion.

Carrying their world across the emptiness

Nomads in Iguidi

Throughout the entire brawl between camel and humans, the Half-Child had been thrusting his little black fist in and out of her vagina. I looked down on the camel panting on the ground. She had had an orgasm.

No one was really interested in the abused camel. She was nothing but a hostage to keep the young one nearby the camp until dinner time. Allah will provide, Omar was fond of saying, and now Allah had provided. We studied the tender piece of living meat with gourmets' eyes.

We did not eat the camel that night. Dermas and el Kiad had not yet returned. It would have been inconceivable to have eaten such a meal without them. They trotted into camp the next day with a third nomad and a pathetic-looking camel, more like a donkey with a hump. The third nomad, setting eyes on the captured camel, looked very happy. For three days he had been searching for them, he said, after he had given thanks to Allah. For the first and last time on my journey, Tahar Omar looked as if he was about to lose faith in his God.

Omar was not only disappointed in God's will; he was disappointed in Dermas' and el Kiad's judgement of camels. What money Omar had made out of selling me *Mr Wilson*, he now lost with this new purchase. More than just money was at stake; it was his pride too. He had lost face in front of a *nasrani*.

Then Dermas, by way of compensation, produced from behind his saddle the backside of a gazelle. It had been shot by the nomads from whom he had bought the camel, and they had given it to him to take back to Omar. Omar let out a burst of merriment and praise for God. In a moment his depression about the camel deal had been forgotten. Omar's knife quickly sliced off steaks, and long before they had properly grilled on the fire, eight pairs of yellowing and decayed nomadic teeth were tearing into them with gusto.

At an earlier time, according to Strabo, the whole of North Africa, from Carthage to the pillars of Hercules, abounded in wild beasts. 'The reason why the name nomads or wanderers was bestowed on these people originated in their not being able to devote themselves to husbandry on account of the wild beasts.'[5]

[5] Strabo, *Geography XVII.*

F

Elephant, giraffe, ostrich, rhino, buffalo, lion, and antelope roamed the Sahara.

What has happened since then is depressingly predictable. Today, gazelle, jackal, and the occasional Addax antelope are the only large animals left. Even they are becoming an increasing rarity as soldiers, nomads, tourists, and 'sportsmen' shoot them down from Land-Rovers with automatic rifles.

The Romans set the example, an example that was to be followed by the vast majority of 'civilized' people after them. To feed the Roman public's insatiable lust for blood, Caesar threw four hundred lions into battle with four hundred gladiators. Later the Emperor Titus celebrated the opening of the Colosseum with nine thousand animals killed. Not to be outdone by his predecessors, the Emperor Trajan slaughtered 2246 animals in one sitting. It is impossible to estimate how many hundreds of thousands of animals died in the ring, or how many millions must have been killed while being captured. But we should be wary of our condemnations. A society that gets its kicks from disaster films and horror movies is hardly in a position to judge too harshly the crowds who flocked to the Colosseum.

Yet right up until 1830, if the picture that Jean-Auguste Margueritte gives in his *Chasses de l'Algérie* is correct, North Africa still abounded in wild game. It was not until the invention of the breech-loading rifle that the killings turned into exterminations. In the last half-century alone, the ostrich, the leopard, and the hartebeest have disappeared. What animals are left, are living on borrowed time. Already the Addax antelope is almost extinct, following one single hunt by French Meharists that turned into an indiscriminate slaughter.

The next day we loaded up to leave. We marched over a bitter, desiccated land. The caravan made no attempt to keep together, and soon I found myself with el Kiad, well ahead of the others. It was quiet and peaceful. In the distance we could hear the far-off shouts of the others calling to each other. We shifted south, then east, then south-south-east. I followed el Kiad through a series of dried-up river beds that had worn their way through the rocky terrain over hundreds of thousands of years, until we came onto a great plain covered with black slate. There el Kiad, like a compass needle wavering first one way then the other, until finally bearing onto course, swung south-east towards Bouir Ikrief.

The wind dropped and the sun was high above our heads. I could feel the heat around me. We were walking across layers of slate, scorching on their surface and razor sharp on their edges. The lifeless surface was devoid of all colour save jet black. We walked in silence. Only able to communicate the simplest of words and phrases, life became a very simple affair. You ate, you slept, you walked, and you drank. Nothing else mattered.

The day wore on and our shadows grew longer. By late afternoon my feet were beginning to ache. But sunset cooled the air and gave me second wind. I walked through the early night enjoying the pleasure of an evening stroll.

After about an hour of night, the plain of black slates came to an end. In front of us was what appeared to be a garden growing out of the desert. I thought of the Koran's description of Paradise. 'The Paradise promised to the righteous is as if rivers flow through it; its fruit is everlasting and also its shade.'[6]

'Water,' el Kiad said, pointing.

I began to walk towards it.

'Stay,' he shouted. 'We must wait for the others before we enter.'

The next morning, after tea, Omar told me that we would be staying by the water-hole for another day because of the richness of the grazing. I was no longer surprised by any delays. I got up and explored the water-hole. The water was low, but a higher watermark showed that the hole had once seen better days. Around the hole were the tracks and droppings of gazelle, lizard, jackal, and desert hare. The grass and the bushes around were crowded with living things. After the silence and deadness of the black slate, it was like a bustling city. Birds chirped in the air and pecked fussily at the ground, while squadrons of black and golden butterflies hovered above the water. The most prominent of all the inhabitants of this ecological city were the grasshoppers. They swarmed through the foliage in their thousands.

[6] *The Koran*, 13:36, trans. Muhammad Zafrulla Khan, London, 1970.

Although the grasshopper and the locust differ in their habits, their colours, and even the structure of their bodies, they belong to the same species. In a rainy season the hopper will multiply in numbers and spread out over fertile areas. After a drought the fertile area will have diminished, so the hoppers will concentrate, develop gregarious habits and breed, laying hundreds of eggs at a time. In three weeks the eggs will have hatched, and in another six weeks the newly-born locusts will have reached maturity and be ready to breed in turn. Locust swarms, devouring all before them, can spread for hundreds of miles. *Exodus* tells how Egypt suffered a drought followed by a plague of locusts.

What I saw at that water-hole were the remains of a larger locust swarm that had been killed off by the continuous drought. They were desperately trying to eke out a living in the fertile areas that were left. As I looked at the swarms of locusts, Omar came up to me. 'The will of God' he said, desolately, and waddled on.

That evening a herd of some fifty camel came down to the water-hole to drink. They marched in perfect order, heads following tails in one long line. There was no nomadic cameleer to urge them on from behind, only a king bull at the front to lead the way. Their movements were governed by a common consent that not even man, in the shape of Omar shouting at them because they were walking over his merchandise, could alter.

A series of minor and unmemorable delays kept us at the water-hole for another day. The cameleer who was responsible for the herd which we had seen that evening had discovered our presence. He negotiated the sale of another camel with Omar as he drank his tea, ate his food, and tried to cadge off his *nasrani*. He hung round the edge of our group like a bad smell that lingers and never goes away, taking but never giving, ingratiating but never helping. He had no tea, he told Omar. Omar gave him tea. He had no sugar, he whined. Omar gave him sugar. Finally Omar turned away from him in disgust.

'He has no dignity,' he said, after he had gone. 'He is not a man.'

This was to be my last day with Lehia, el Kiad, 'Mood and

Kahil. From here we would all be going our separate ways. El Kiad and his son Mohammed were going west to do business with some Rguibat kinsmen. Lehia, 'Mood and Kahil were returning to Chegga. Omar, Dermas, the Half-Child, and myself were going on to Taoudenni.

The next morning we were loading up to go when Kahil interrupted us with a shout. Two men on camels were galloping towards us. 'Mood and Mohammed raised their rifles with unconvincing melodrama. One of the camel-riders shouted out the beginnings of the salutation. Omar took it up. The rifles were not necessary, Omar motioned, so 'Mood and Mohammed lowered them with disappointment. The visitors were friends; they did not falter over the phrases.

As everyone went through the customary salutations, I saw two pairs of eyes observing me through indigo-blue veils. They were watching me with a mixture of irony and curiosity. Omar explained to them that I was a *nasrani* on my way to Taoudenni, and that I came from a country that was ruled by a woman. You would expect them to pity me in such a situation, but they didn't. They roared with laughter. As they laughed, I noticed that one of the newcomers had only half a right foot. I asked him why. He had lost the other half in a fight with a camel, he answered.

Omar sent off the Half-Child to find the cameleer and announced that there would be a feast. Departure was delayed for yet another day.

The Half-Child returned with the cameleer and a baby camel. A fire was built up and the cameleer, at the chance of free meat, made himself at home by the fire. This time Omar didn't mind. He was welcome. Everyone was welcome. I could no longer grudge Omar the money he had made out of the sale of *Mr Wilson*. He was a rogue, but a generous rogue. The young camel that we were to eat had cost him a lot of money. I thought how gracious nomads are in their welcome, and how generous in their hospitality.

As we drank tea, Dermas led the condemned camel away to the place of execution, a cluster of rocks nearby. The camel was dragged along struggling. It was as if he already knew the fate that was awaiting him. The rest of the camp finished their tea and then walked over to join Dermas.

Mohammed produced a penknife for the killing but it was too small. Omar brought out his dagger but it was too blunt. Finally a use was found for my ridiculous sheath knife of heroic proportions. El Kiad took the knife from me, pointed the victim's head towards Mecca, and expertly inserted it into the throat, like a doctor injecting a patient.

The young camel gave a shudder and a fountain of blood spurted out of its neck. El Kiad took the knife out and the flow of blood rapidly increased. Gallons came out, completely flooding the rock holes around. Soon the blood overflowed the rock pools and trickled down the rocks in miniature waterfalls. The camel was still alive, but every line in its body seemed to have altered. It moaned, quivered, and shuddered in pain. As the life-force in it shrank, so the muscles in its body seemed to have tightened. The camel was taking a very long time to die. At last, summoning up all its remaining strength, it made one last unsuccessful lurch back to life, soaking everyone with its blood. It breathed deeply and then sank down to its death, its foreleg on the right side twitching hopelessly.

The killing was followed by the cutting. First the legs were stretched out and skinned. Then the hump was split open and the skin on either side of it was rolled back. Next the nomads tore the rib-cage out. Behind the rib-cage was a green balloon full of evil smelling liquid. Dermas carefully took it out and deposited it several feet away from us. Omar held his nose.

'You may have to drink that if there is no water, *Nasrani*,' he shouted gleefully and cruelly.

Everyone joined in the skinning. The dead flesh was cold and slippery and our hands were covered in blood. But it was innocent blood. And we were innocent too. We had killed for food, not for sport.

As everyone waited for the meat to cook, the gossip of the desert was exchanged and the politics of the tribes were discussed. The main topic of conversation was the Spanish Sahara and the sudden escalation in Morocco's demands for the territory. The two newcomers talked of rifles that had been taken across the

border into 'Spain'. One of them told the nomads of the power
of these magnificent guns.

'They fire and fire again and again without being reloaded.
Bang—bang—bang—bang.'

'*Automatique*,' said Omar knowledgeably.

'*Beserf*. Too much,' the nomads exclaimed at this news.

Only Omar was against the threatening war. He said it would
be bad for business. The others, especially 'Mood, were already
fantasizing about how many Moroccans they would kill. 'Mood
was waving his rifle around, miming future battles.

When the meat had cooked, the talk of war evaporated. The
entire company attacked the meal. It began with the kidneys and
went on well into the night. We ate, we slept, and then we ate
again. Nothing was wasted. Our stomachs became bloated and
our bodies immovable.

I woke again in the small hours of the morning. Clouds
covered the sky and I could no longer see any stars. There was a
roar of thunder. I felt a drop of rain strike me, and then another,
and another. The rain was striking everything. I could hear the
roar of thunder. I looked around me at the nomads sleeping it off.
I imagined that the rain would wake them and they would dance
around overjoyed. But none of them moved. I don't think they
even felt the rain . . . or if they did feel it, then they didn't
notice it . . . or if they noticed it, then they didn't care about it.

4

The Taghaza Road

We left the following afternoon, 18 November, with that heavy Boxing Day feeling. Now there was only Omar, Dermas, the Half-Child, and myself. We were walking across a bare plain of sand and rocks beneath a scattering of thin and worthless clouds. The sands had quickly drunk up what rain had fallen the previous night, and everything was dry and lifeless. Yet in spite of the landscape, the barrenness, and the overloaded midriff I was in a state of exhilaration. Above us the two buzzards played dog-fights in the sky, bringing us good luck, like albatrosses following a ship.

This sense of movement did not last however. It never lasted. Just as I was about to sing with joy and praise Allah for giving us speed, there would be sudden chaos, and the emptiness around would be filled with the groans of a collapsed camel, his spindly legs splayed out at right angles. When that happened, Dermas would run up to the camel and Omar would shout at me to do the same. I would hold the camel's halter while Dermas readjusted the load. When the camel was up, we would set off once again to Taoudenni.

The third time that this happened, I ran up to the collapsed camel too abruptly and his neighbour tried to bolt. Omar motioned me to the head of the caravan and sent the Half-Child back to help his father.

'*Nasrani*,' he shouted, 'you are useless with camels. You do not only do nothing, you do harm. When you run up to a camel, you cause more trouble, not less. You are too abrupt in your ways and you scare them. I know why,' he said, tapping his head with a finger, 'it is because you are frightened of the camels. You are! Do not pretend that you are not. I have been watching you. From now on you will remain at the front of the caravan in the boy's place. When we stop and have to reload a camel, study the boy carefully and see how it is done. Study carefully.'

He threw the camel's headrope at me and told me to walk.

'Be careful, *Nasrani*. Here you will have to change your ways.'

I will never forget those hours that I spent leading the caravan through the Erg Cherch Desert. It was hardly the punishment that Omar intended it to be. I walked across the empty desert day with nothing to distract me except the endless shimmering horizons and unlimited expanses of blue sky. Behind me, Omar, high on his white bull, set a course as a pilot would directing a helmsman in an unfamiliar sea.

'A little to the right.'

'Steady now.'

'Keep on that course.'

'Concentrate, *Nasrani*, concentrate.'

By late afternoon the plain of sand and stones had given way to a stretch of gravel that left soft sand marks on your footprints. With dusk the gravel turned into grit. Walking over this flat plain of grit I felt reduced in stature against the immensity around, as in a dream.

'I said concentrate, *Nasrani*, concentrate.'

'Slow down a little. You are going too fast.'

'Just keep that slab of rock over there on your left eye and walk forward.'

'Now slow a little, *Nasrani*, slow. Easy, easy.'

'Easy, easy' was a favourite expression of Omar's. Sometimes he said it to himself. More often he said it to me.

We walked through the early hours of the night until the way ahead was abruptly blocked by a range of sand dunes.

'We will stop here,' said Omar. 'The camels must rest.'

When we had unloaded and hobbled the camels, Omar ordered the Half-Child and myself to search around for the dried-up roots that we used for fuel. The grit was almost totally barren. After half an hour we returned with just about enough to make a miser's fire.

'A good place?' I asked Omar.

'No, it is not a good place. Look around, *Nasrani*. Is there food for the camels? No, there is nothing. It is a very bad place. But the camels are tired. They cannot cross these dunes tonight. So we must stay here, even though there is nothing to eat for the animals and nothing to burn for our food.'

'The will of God,' I said, trying to think of something intelligent to say.

Omar spat out some phlegm.

'What does a *nasrani* know about the will of God?'

Morning was bitter cold. For six hours we hauled ourselves over those endless crescent-shaped dunes. They rolled away as far as the horizon and beyond it. We tacked our way across them in a zig-zag course, as yachtsmen do when they sail into a headwind. From a distance the dunes looked supremely sensual, like women's breasts. But close up their beauty was deceptive. They had two sides; on the windward side the slopes were hard, the sand packed firm and tight. On the other side the sand was soft; it was loose and unstable and fell away as you tried to put your feet in it, burying you up to your thighs and scalding your legs with its burning heat.

The camels knew the dangers of these sinking sands by instinct. As we crossed the dunes they became tense and unmanageable, and had to be coaxed through them very slowly. Time-consuming and energy-consuming precautions had to be taken to ensure that they would not fall down the slopes into the soft sand and break their legs. Sometimes the entire caravan had to be unloaded, and we would have to carry the baggage piece by piece across the burning sands so that the camels could cross unhindered.

Every so often Omar would send the Half-Child scampering up to the crests of a dune to report to Omar on the layout of the land ahead. When the boy had reached the top, Omar would bark out a series of questions to him. Omar could tell, by the colour of the sand, the texture of the slopes we had to cross, and he would plot our way accordingly.

Early in the afternoon we came to a short break in the dunes. Men and mounts were exhausted. Around us was a plain of grit with the occasional patch of green on it. Beyond the grit was

another range of dunes. Omar raised his right hand, giving the
signal to stop. We hissed at our camels until they flopped down
onto their haunches and, for the last time that day, unloaded the
baggage onto the sand.

Though impatient to reach Taoudenni, I was glad that the day
had ended. True, I had been warned by the Sous-Préfet that the
day would be hard, but I never expected it to be quite so hard.
We finished the unloading and sat by the fire. As we waited for
Omar to brew tea, I noticed hundreds of maggots crawling over
the remains of the camel that we had slaughtered two days
earlier.

I pointed them out to Omar.

He looked at me astonished.

'Of course there are maggots in the meat. There are always
maggots in meat.'

Two more soul-destroying and back-breaking days crossing
those dunes followed. Whenever possible, Omar avoided the soft
sand, keeping us on the hard crests. The sands were scorching hot.
Only the surface of a dune, which is made up of millions of tiny
particles of sand, is exposed to the sun. Because of the tightly-
packed particles of sand, the heat cannot penetrate, so the heat of
the dunes is localized on the surface. This accounts for the intense
heat of the dunes. During the battle of Metarfa, the Arab foot-
soldiers were slaughtered because the dunes were so hot that
they couldn't lie down to take cover. Dunes have been known to
reach a temperature of 158°F.

It needed all Omar's and Dermas's skills as cameleers to get the
caravan through the dunes. On the crest of each dune we held the
camels' headropes tight to stop them plunging down into the
sinking sands. There were times, however, when the caravan
could not avoid these sands. So we would unload the caravan, dig
a pathway through the sand and lead the camels down, one by
one.

Once a camel missed its foothold and rolled down the steep
side of the dune. It landed in the soft sand on its side, and slowly
began to sink, as if in quicksand. Omar and Dermas raced down
the dune, shouting at me to follow, while the Half-Child soothed
the other camels. We tumbled down to the panic-stricken camel

and dug frantically around him, while Omar pulled at the head-rope, leaning over with all his weight. After about five minutes of supreme effort, the camel was free. Miraculously not one leg had been broken.

We spent three days in those dunes, the last day being the hardest of all. The sun beat down like a silent hammer on our heads. The last dune that we encountered was the worst of all. It looked almost uncrossable. First we dug a path about a hundred yards long with our hands and knees. Then we unloaded the baggage, hauling each piece across the sands separately. Finally we led the camels along the path. The camels were intensely suspicious. Either they refused to move, or they panicked, falling down into the soft sand below. In the end they had to be dragged across the sand one at a time, like the baggage. It took over three hours, in the heat of the early afternoon, to travel that last hundred yards.

On the other side of the dunes we found ourselves on a multi-coloured plain of stones and shingles. Reds, blues, greens, whites, and purples haphazardly patterned the desert floor. We crossed purple wadis and sky-blue hills, skirted ridges of coral red, and rode over carpets of yellow shingle. As evening fell, the plain narrowed into a bottleneck. It was being pushed in by buttes that broke up the horizon like skyscrapers, and it ended up in a canyon.

'We will camp here,' said Omar. 'Tomorrow, *Inshallah*, Bouir Ikrief.'

I slept little that night. My bones were aching from the labours in the dunes, and the cold nights had given me severe backache. The puncture in the sleeping bag had got larger. Each day I lost more feathers, and each night I lost more sleep.

I spent most of the night lying on my side, staring at the dying embers of the fire. Occasionally one of the others would get up and warm himself by what was left of the embers, and then go back to sleep again. The bitter cold kept them awake. They had only blankets, and were only able to sleep in snatches.

I woke early the next morning. An aching back on a mattress of pebbles encourages an early rising. We marched well that morning. Bouir Ikrief, the first target of our journey, was within reach. We made our way through the canyon and back onto the plain of coloured pebbles. Only the sudden squawking of the two buzzards disturbed the silence, as they laboured low overhead, their outstretched wings casting contorted shadows on the canyon's walls.

The coloured pebbles covered the ground like a Persian carpet. An hour further on the colours disappeared, and we were on a plain of black and grey slate. Somewhere among those slates lay Bouir Ikrief, the last watering place before Taoudenni, reputed to have the sweetest water on the Taghaza Road. I would not have known that we had reached it if Omar hadn't pointed it out to me. All there was to mark it was a faded brown circle of camel dung that intensified towards the centre and fell away into a hole that was covered by slates.

'For hundreds of years the caravans have used Bouir Ikrief,' Omar said to me. 'Thousands and thousands of camels have passed this way,' he went on, as Dermas uncovered the waterhole.

I contemplated the brown mound that Omar was sitting on. The Taghaza Road had been travelled down since the eleventh century. Just think of it, what Omar was sitting on was nine hundred years of camel shit.

We hobbled the camels and prepared to water them. As we lined up the camels, I saw Omar cut a piece of camel shit off the mound that he was sitting on and make a fire to brew tea. I shook my head with hopelessness. We were well into the second half of November. A journey that Omar had confidently predicted would take four days had ended up taking sixteen. According to Omar's original reckoning, we should be just getting into Taoudenni by now. Like Alexander Kinglake, I was no longer impressed by the Children of Israel's forty years wandering in the desert. By nomad standards it was a normal schedule.

Watering the camels was a long and drawn-out process, and I was glad of the tea-break in the middle. When the camels were finally satisfied and the waterskins had been filled, we walked another two miles across the slates until we came to a little grass underneath a tree. There we camped for three days, resting

ourselves and our camels, in preparation for the long trek without
water to Taoudenni.

It was during those three days that Omar told me about the long
lines of men and camels that used to journey up and down the
Taghaza Road. He spoke of caravans of thousands of camels that
went down to Timbuktu bearing cloth, and he spoke of the long
lines of black slaves that went up to Morocco in exchange. He
told me of bandits, too, who, before the French arrived, lay in
wait for the caravans at the water-holes on the Taghaza Road.
He was like some old historic monument. I asked him when all
this was, but he could not answer. It was sometime in the vague
and unmeasurable past, when he was younger than I am now.
That was all he would say. Years were as meaningless as days to
Omar.

The Taghaza Road was once the most important caravan route
in North Africa. From Leo Africanus we can get a clear picture
of the trade that passed along the road. He wrote of merchants
doing 'a great traffic in the land of the Negroes'. The principal
goods taken south were cloth, sugar, brass vessels, horses, books,
and salt. These were exchanged for gold, slaves, and civet. Leo
describes one caravan made up entirely of produce that came out
of the Soudan.

> Fiftie men slaves and fiftie women slaves brought out of the
> land of the Negros, tenne eunuchs, twelve camels, one Giraffa,
> sixteene civet-cats, one pound of civet, a pound of amber, and
> almost six hundred skins of a certaine beast called by them
> Elamt whereof they make their shieldes, everie skin being
> worth at Fez eight ducates, twentie of the men slaves cost
> twentie ducates a peece, and so did fifteene of the women
> slaves; every eunuch was valued at fortie, every camel at
> fiftie, and every civet-cat at two hundred ducats; and a pound
> of civet and amber is solde at Fez for three score ducates.[1]

> In the confused and ill-documented history of North Africa,
> of the Sahara and of the countries to the north and to the south,
> there runs a golden thread [wrote E. W. Bovill]. From the

[1] Africanus, *op. cit.*, Vol. III.

Nile Valley in the east to the Atlantic in the west there was
trafficking in gold with the interior of Africa at all times in
recorded history. Slaves and gold, gold and slaves, provided
the lifeblood of the trade of the Maghrib with the Sudan. The
gold flowed in two main streams, the Garamantian road, from
the Fezzan to Tripoli, and the Taghaza road from the Niger to
Sijilmasa in Morocco; the one in the east and the other in the
west. The flow seems to have been steady but not spectacular.
There were occasions, however, when the world caught a
fleeting glimpse of gold in quantities which clearly betrayed
fabulous wealth hidden away in the interior. Early in the
fourteenth century Mansu Musa emerged dramatically from
the desert to astonish Egypt and the western world by his
prodigal display of gold. Two centuries and a half later the
Moors of Morocco so enriched themselves with gold by
conquering the countries of the Middle Niger that an
obsequious Christendom competed with the Turks for the
favours of their sultan. Where the gold came from was a
problem which Christian and Muslim tried unceasingly to
solve, and a quest which inspired some of the great exploits in
the history of geographical discovery. But so secretive were
all those engaged in the trade that the solution was not found
until very recent times. [2]

Black Africa was totally lacking in salt. So great was the
negroes' desire for it that they exchanged it for gold, often
weight for weight. It was a mysterious trade, and it only existed
because of the West and Central African's insatiable demand for
salt. But it made fortunes for the Arabs who engaged in it.
According to the seventeenth-century chronicler known as
'Ro. C.':

[The Salt was taken] to a kind of deformed Negro, who will
never be seene in the commerce of trading with the Barbarian
or any stranger. Wherefore they lay their salt in the fields and
leaveth it, then cometh the deformed Negro, and layeth against
every man's pricell of salt, as much of his gold as he thinks the
salt is worth, and goeth his way, leaving his gold with the salt;

[2] Bovill, *op. cit.*

Then returneth the Moor, if he like the gold, taketh it away, if not, detracteth so much from his heap, as he will sell to the Negro for his gold. The Negro returneth, if he like the quantity putteth too more gold, or else will not barter, but departeth. Yet they seldom mislike, for the Moore maketh a rich return, and his king a full treasure, Wherefore the deformed Negro is praised for the truest dealing man in the world.[3]

The source of the gold remained a mystery that not even the Moors could penetrate. Once they captured one of these 'deformed Negroes' and tortured him to try to find out where the gold came from. The 'deformed Negro', probably a pigmy, died without speaking. The mystery of the gold was not solved until 1960, when two members of the University of Ghana, J. J. Scarisbrick and P. C. Carter, visited Buré, on the western border of Ghana.

At Buré they found primitive gold mines that were exploited by methods that had remained unchanged for nearly a thousand years. They found parallel rows of holes about two and a half feet in diameter and three feet apart. Inside the ground the holes were joined up by grids of tunnels that had undermined large areas in the inside of the hillsides. The miners worked in teams. One team hacked out the gold with small picks; another team floated the calabashes of earth and gold down the flooded tunnels. Then a third and a fourth team purified the gold, washing it in water.

'This is apparently as it has always been,' wrote Scarisbrick and Carter. 'This was how the gold was mined through the medieval empires of Mali and Ghana, across the Sahara to, say, Sijilmasa, from Sijilmasa to, say, Ceuta; from Ceuta to, say, Genoa; from Genoa to heaven knows where.'[4]

The trade in gold continued, with the Arabs jealously safeguarding their position as middle-men. Europe was becoming increasingly interested in the gold. Trade in general was

[3] Ro. C. (believed to be Capt. Robert Coverts), *A True Historical Discourse of Muley Hamet's rising to the three Kingdomes of Moruecos, Fes and Sus*, London, 1609.

[4] J. J. Scarisbrick and P. L. Carter, 'An Expedition to Wangara', *Ghana Notes and Queries*, No. *1*, 1961.

increasing, and by the fourteenth century gold was urgently needed as a currency in the newly-developed capitalist Europe. A series of wars and an increase in trade used up all Europe's gold reserves. The new merchants of Italy turned to Africa for more gold.

It was at this time that the first European attempt to find the source of the gold was embarked upon. Antonio Malfante, a Genoese merchant travelling in disguise, penetrated to the middle of the Sahara before having to turn back. He repeatedly asked an old sheikh, who knew the Soudan well, where the gold came from. And he always got the same answer. 'I spent fourteen years in the negro country and I never heard of, or saw, a man who could say with certain knowledge "This is what I saw, this is how they find and collect the gold".'[5]

It was at this same time that the Taghaza Road was first mentioned on European maps, usually inaccurately. On the well-known *Catalan Atlas* of Charles V, drawn by Abraham Cresques, is a picture of a monarch seated on a throne. 'This negro lord,' the inscription reads, 'is called Musa Mali, Lord of the Negroes of Guinea. So abundant is the gold which is found in his country that he is the richest and most noble king in all the land.'

In the eighteenth century the trade in gold began to decline. It was replaced by the trade in slaves. At the height of the slave trade, Africans were being taken out of the Soudan at the rate of a hundred thousand a year. If you accept Dr Livingstone's estimate that ten slaves died for every one that reached the coast, the number of Africans taken as slaves is astronomical. By 1900 large areas of the Soudan had been totally depopulated. The liberal consciences of the West may have objected, but the men who took the slaves across, men like Omar's father, had nothing to fear. They knew every water-hole on the Taghaza Road. All they had to do was to point the way to the next well and the long column of black zombies would trudge forward.

Slavery may have been a moral issue, but it was an economic solution. For who but slaves would pick the tobacco of Virginia, cultivate the sugar of Barbados, work the silver mines of South

[5] Quoted in A. da Cadamosto, *Voyages*, ed. and trans. G. R. Crone, London, 1937.

G

America, or dig the salt of Taoudenni? Bristol is still rich on the trade in slaves.

It was in the interests of these labour merchants that the slaves were in good condition by the time they reached the coast. So the slavers built camps where the slaves who survived the journey could be fed and rested, before they were sold on the markets for profits of up to five hundred per cent.

An important and particularly vile aspect of this trade was the traffic in eunuchs, who were in large demand as the guardians of harems. In order to foster this lucrative trade, some African tribes, particularly the Mossi, would punish criminals with castration. The Mossi were famed for their skill at this type of operation, and kept their methods a closely-guarded secret. The purpose of the operation was to allow the eunuch to perform sexual intercourse without making any of the harem pregnant. Many of the harem owners objected; so the Mossi perfected another type of operation that completely mutilated the member. Less than ten per cent of the potential eunuchs survived this operation.

Yet Europe is hardly in a position to condemn. Child-prostitution and sexual mutilations were common in Victorian England. Right up until the end of the nineteenth century, the 'Soprani' of the Papal Choir were all eunuchs.

René Caillié, the first European to return from Timbuktu alive, travelled on one such slave caravan.

Our caravan was numerous: it consisted of fourteen hundred camels, laden with the various productions of the Soudan; as gold, slaves, ivory, gum, ostrich-feathers and cloth in the piece and made into dresses. [It was] a perfect tumult of men and beasts.

The oldest caravan conductors go first, to lead the way. A sand-hill, a rock, a difference of colour in the sand, a few tufts of herbage are infallible marks which enable them to recognize their situation.

The further northward we proceeded the more barren the country became. The plain had the precise appearance of the ocean; perhaps such as the bed of a sea would have if left by the water. In fact, the winds form in the sands undulating furrows like the waves of the sea.[6]

In 1828, when Caillié made his journey, the trans-Saharan caravan trade was at its peak. But as the nineteenth century wore on, it went into decline. In 1892 Timbuktu and the Soudan fell to the French, who built a railway line from the Niger to the Atlantic. In 1902 Kano, in northern Nigeria, was occupied by the British, who built a railway line to Lagos. Not only did the caravans lose to the railways, but the new colonial governments put on heavy pressure to halt the trade in 'Black Ivory'. Oscar Lenz saw one of the last of the large slave caravans pass through Tindouf, with Bambara slaves, at the end of the nineteenth century, but the trade continued for many years on a smaller scale. It was not until the French capture of Tindouf in 1935 that the trans-Saharan slave traffic could be said to have come to an end.

With the new economic and political system imposed by the French, came a new type of transport. In 1923 the first trans-Saharan motor-crossing was made by Citroen half-tracks.

'Of all the innovations introduced by the French in the Sahara,' wrote Capot-Rey, a Frenchman, 'none, not even the peace nor the multiplication of wells, have had such a profound effect on the conditions of life as the motor-car; to discover a fact of comparable importance one must go back to the domestication of the camel.'[7]

Sitting at our camp at Bouir Ikrief, thinking these things, I watched the grazing camels with their ugly elongated necks. They reminded me of dinosaurs, wending their way through the dawn of history (whenever that was) towards extinction. I thought of Omar and his fellow nomads, so close to those camels and so reliant on them, and I dearly hoped that they, like their camels, would not become obsolete.

We planned to leave after only two days at Bouir Ikrief, but on our second morning we found that one of the camels had strayed

[6] Caillié, op. cit.
[7] R. Capot-Rey, Le Sahara français, Paris, 1953.

during the night. It took a day for Dermas to find him. He went off in search of the camel in the early morning. At midday he was not back. By late afternoon he still had not returned. By evening Omar was clearly worried.

He directed the Half-Child and myself to break off branches from the nearby tree. We dragged these up the granite escarpment that ran along one horizon, and built a great fire, visible for miles around. We cooked and ate our meal on the top of the escarpment, sheltering from the wind where we could. We ate in silence, staring into the black infinity of the night, our eyes searching for Dermas. Every so often we would shout out into the darkness, in the hope that Dermas might hear. It was a faint hope. If he did not return by morning, Omar said, then we would have to go in search of him.

He finally appeared just as we were about to sleep. The lost camel had broken free from his hobbling ropes and wandered around for miles. Dermas had followed the camel's tracks for over ten hours before he caught him. All the time Dermas had been on foot.

'*La bas*. No evil,' said Omar.

'*La bas, Hamdullah*. No evil, thanks to God,' replied Dermas.

We left the next morning, marching into the headwind, dragging our camels behind us.

The wind blew in gusts, almost bowling us over. We were moving parallel to the granite escarpment on our right. It had turned the wind straight at us. We travelled with it for about ten miles, until it gradually fell away, the wind correcting its direction and the land opening up into a flat plain.

As the escarpment disappeared over our shoulders, Omar pointed at the renegade camel.

'We have lost a day because of him,' he growled. 'Tomorrow we will have to make up two days in one.'

I listened to his newly-found concern for speed and efficiency without belief, and walked on without another thought for the next day.

Then suddenly Omar's white bull, which was a little to one side of me, stopped. He braced his hindlegs for a pee and I vaguely saw a gush of camel's urine hit the ground. A second later, without warning, there was a powerful gust of wind. I was drenched. With no more water until Taoudenni, I thought philosophically, I would just have to get used to the smell. I raised my eyes to the sky to offer my sufferings up to Allah. All I saw were the two buzzards squawking with laughter above me.

We walked in silence until we were abruptly interrupted by a shout from behind. All four of us turned to look. A man on a camel was galloping towards us. We could see him clearly, his indigo-blue robes standing out against the khaki landscape around. He galloped right up to us. Just as he was about to crash into the caravan, he pulled his camel to a halt.

'*Salam alaikum*,' he said through the folds of his head-dress.

'*Alaikum wa salam*,' Omar replied.

I thought of Scobie in Laurence Durrell's *Cleo*.

They're regular Britishers for politeness, my boy. No good throwing your '*Salam Alaikum*' around just anyhow. It must be given first by a camel-rider to a man on a horse, by a horse-man to a man on a donkey, by a donkey-rider to a man on foot, by a man on foot to a man seated, by a small party to a large one, by the younger to the older. . . . It's only in the great schools at home they teach such things. But here every nipper has it at his finger's end.[8]

I could not see the newcomer's face; it was hidden by his headgear to protect it from the wind. Yet the build of the man looked very familiar. My eyes wandered over him, from his turban, to his saddle, to his right foot. He was familiar. Half the right foot was missing.

There and then Omar ordered us to hobble the camels and build a fire. When the fire was built we squatted round while Omar made tea. As tea was being brewed the nomads discussed the gossip of the desert. The Spanish Sahara was still the main topic of conversation. The newcomer told us how he was on his way to some kinsmen and from there he would be going with them into 'Spain'. He had seen our tracks in the sand, and, rather than stop at Bouir Ikrief, he had come over to see us straightaway.

[8] Laurence Durrell, *Cleo*, London, 1960.

He talked of 'Spain' with all the enthusiasm of a 1914 recruit expecting to be home by Christmas.

'Guns, many of them . . . Guns that go bang-bang-bang-bang, and do not need to be reloaded. With these guns we will kill many, many Moroccans. Too much.'

Omar listened to him in silence, and from the deep recesses of my memory a conversation from childhood came back to me.

'And the others, the Somalis?'

'If you ask a Somali he'll simply say "We've had a white ruler replaced by a black one".'

I remember at first being surprised that so much of the nomad's aggression should be directed against Morocco. True, the Moroccans were the traditional enemy of the desert nomad, but was not Spain the colonial power? Then I recalled the evening drone of Tahar Omar's radio. The Spanish had responded to Morocco's territorial claims by developing a crude Saharan nationalism. The slogans 'Neither Moroccan, nor Mauritanian nor Algerian' and 'The Sahara is Saharan' were endlessly repeated on the Spanish 'Radio Sahara'. This served its purpose at the time, creating an image of a benevolent Spain protecting the desert nomad from the expansionist ambitions of Morocco. But later, when a genuine nationalist movement emerged, this propaganda backfired. 'Neither Moroccan, nor Mauritanian, nor Algerian' and 'The Sahara is Saharan' became slogans of the Polisario Front.

A wave of anger swept over me at the way these nomads were being so callously used by the Spanish. I looked at the Rguibat who had been enthusing about the automatic weapons, the news of which had spread across so many encampments, then I looked at Omar.

'Have you ever heard of the Crusade of Children, Omar?'

'Did the Spanish organize that, too?'

Why was it that Omar always managed to be thirty seconds ahead of me?

We sat talking and drinking tea for over an hour. Then abruptly, as abruptly as he had arrived, the newcomer rose from his haunches, said goodbye, offered us the peace of God, mounted his camel, and rode away towards Bouir Ikrief. He was the last human being whom we were to see until we reached Taoudenni.

We camped that night by a dried-up water-hole. Omar told me the name of it, but I have forgotten. There was grazing there, but the only sign of animal wild life, a lizard, took one look at us, stuck out his tongue, and darted away in fright.

I dreamt that night of a childhood holiday on the south coast of England. I was climbing up a white cliff. From the beach below I could hear the voices of grown-ups.

'Come down this instant. Come down.'

'I can't. I can't.'

'Come down the way you got up.'

'But I can't. I can't.'

I had been keeping a dream diary and I noted that none of my dreams were about the Present. Each night my unconscious pulled me back struggling into my Past, to some almost forgotten event in childhood. This, I discovered, was by no means unique.

During the entire trip [Jung wrote about his East African journey], my dreams stubbornly followed the tactic of ignoring Africa. They drew exclusively upon scenes from home, and thus seemed to say that they considered—if it is permissible to personify the unconscious processes to this extent—the African journey not as something real, but rather as a symptomatic or symbolic act. . . .

This curious behaviour of my dreams corresponds, incidentally, to a phenomenon which I had noted during the First World War. Soldiers in the field dreamt far less of the war than of their homes. Military psychiatrists considered it a basic principle that a man should be pulled out of the front lines when he started dreaming too much of war scenes, for that meant he no longer possessed any psychic defences against the impressions from outside.[9]

The following day was the hardest I ever encountered. It started in the early hours of half-light. We packed up our camp and left, travelling as far as we could before the full force of the sun came down on us. We travelled fast for two hours, the cold kept us on

[9] Karl Jung, *Memories, Dreams and Reflections*, London, 1967.

the move, and then, as we came to our first obstacle, a range of sand dunes, the heat of the sun fell down on us, a rush of fire from heaven.

With Omar acting as our pilot we made our way up gullies, through valleys, down dry glaciers and under overhanging cliffs—all made out of sand, each feature carved into strange and wonderful shapes by the ever-blowing wind. By the time we came out of the dunes, it was high noon. The glare of the sun was blinding, the sand was burning my feet, and the spittle in my mouth was so thick I could almost chew it.

We found ourselves on a parched plain, totally featureless apart from a clutter of rocks that lay in the sand like the droppings of the gods. We marched across the plain with indifference. Above us the sun rained down. Each foot overtook the other mechanically. After two hours marching, the plain gave way to a white table that looked as if it were made out of papier-mâché. It was the first salt-pan that I had seen.

We began to walk across it. With each step the crusty surface gave way under us. Underneath the crust of salt the ground was damp. Even Omar was obliged to dismount from his camel and walk, searching for the hard patches of crust to tread on. Once he slipped and sank to his knees in a dull white quicksand, and Dermas and myself had to pull him out. I couldn't help smiling a little, as Omar stood knee-deep in quicksand, shouting for assistance. Omar off his camel was as graceless as a grounded bird.

I imagined that we would rest when we reached the end of the salt-pan, but we walked on, across a plain of stones and sand, down a defile, then onto another plain of stones and sand. By mid-afternoon, I estimated, we had already marched over twenty miles.

All that I wanted to do was rest. But rest meant mutiny, and mutiny was unthinkable. I set myself targets to keep on going: a stone to reach, the next thousand paces to count. Thinking about it now, it seems a very childish thing to have done. But it kept my mind occupied, and it stopped me asking Omar that inevitable question: When do we stop?

My legs ached and the heat was hard to bear. Increasingly my progress was becoming a matter of the immediate and the particular: a stone to tread on here, a patch of soft sand to avoid there. Soon I stopped counting the next thousand paces. A thousand paces were too much to conceive of.

Finally I could restrain myself no longer.

'When do we stop?'

Omar looked at me as if I had committed the ultimate social indiscretion. Being with Omar was like being in the very best social circles. It was considered vulgar to ask too many questions.

'Not yet, *Nasrani*. Not yet.'

We went on into the night until we could see no more than a hundred paces in front of us. After two hours of darkness we came upon a range of mountains, their peaks vaguely silhouetted against the light of the quarter moon. I expected Omar to give that silent signal with his hand that meant we were to hobble and unload the camels. He didn't. Instead he led us through a pass so narrow that we had to lead our camels through in single file.

It was hard travelling. A camel collapsed. Omar tried to beat it to its feet, but it would not rise. Silently Dermas came up. He whispered into the camel's ear like a child talking to a favourite pet, gently coaxing it to its feet.

We were deep into the night by the time we reached our camp. Nearby was a well. The ground was littered with camel dung. I dismounted from my camel to drink.

'You cannot drink here,' Omar shouted. 'The water is full of salt. You will go mad.'

I hobbled and unloaded my camel and helped Dermas unload the others. When the work was finished, Omar sat down to prepare the food. I collapsed onto my back exhausted. Night was reduced to a dark tunnel and I did not emerge from that tunnel until I was awoken by the call to prayers the next morning.

René Caillié had gone through a similar experience travelling through the same terrain a hundred and fifty years earlier.

About nine at night, we again decamped and took a north-west direction, as we had done from seven until ten in the morning. Towards midnight, we changed our course to N.N.E. through the passes of high mountains of granite, amongst which were pools of salt water. Enormous masses of these rocks, suspended over our heads, seemed to threaten to tumble and crush us. In one of these defiles, the camel that I rode took fright, turned aside and ran away. I was thrown flat on my back upon the gravel. . . .

To issue from these defiles, we were obliged to climb a steep and lofty mountain; the path was narrow and winding, and presented considerable difficulties, in consequence of which all the company was required to alight from their camels. I alone continued to ride; I was so severely bruised that I should have found it impossible to walk any part of the way. This exposed me to numerous invectives from some of the Moors, who threatened to throw stones at me to compel me to dismount; those, however, who had witnessed my accident took my part, and I was allowed to proceed in peace.

The camels, exhausted by the fatigue of the journey, advanced with reluctance, took two or three steps, then stopped, painfully turning their heads, first on one side and then on the other, uttering low moans, while they seemed to measure with their eyes the laborious task which still remained to be accomplished. It was with regret that I found myself obliged to continue mounted, for I pitied these unfortunate animals. The Moors, walking behind, encouraged them with their voices, repeating certain words in different tones, in the way of a song, which the camels appeared to understand.

The track frequently passed so near the edge of the rock, and was so narrow, that I thought it impossible to follow it without being thrown down frightful precipices. At length, having with great toil attained the summit, we discovered an extensive plain, the soil of which is very hard and interspersed with thin flat stones, resembling slates, and of a grey and black colour.[10]

Next morning I could hardly move. I dreaded the day ahead.

'We will rest the camels here for a day,' Omar said unexpectedly. 'We shall leave tomorrow.'

I remember little about the day, except lying on my back, content with the sheer pleasure of doing nothing. Omar baked

[10] Caillié, *op. cit.*, Vol. II.

bread, Dermas repaired his plastic sandals with a piece of hide, the Half-Child watched over the camels, and I played with Omar's radio until I found Bach's Mass on the B.B.C.'s Overseas Service.

'*Dona Nobis Pacem*,' the radio sang. Lord, give us peace.

The evening is clearer in detail. I remember, as we ate our meal, Dermas pointing at a pair of ears and eyes listening and watching us from behind a rock. It was a jackal. It sat there still and silent, less than twenty yards from our camp fire.

'*Zeeb*,' Omar said to me, giving it its Arabic name. Then he turned to the Half-Child. 'Bring the camels in closer.'

'Jackals do not attack camels, surely?' I said.

'It has happened.'

The next morning we examined the jackals' tracks. There had been two of them. They had encircled the camp three times and then wandered off into the wilderness.

The days that followed, across range after range of sand dunes, telescoped into one another. Each day began with a bitter battleship-grey sky, and sand as cold as snow. After only three hours the sands would heat up under the sun, scorching my calves and feet. This slow, soul-destroying slog through the bulging sand dunes lasted for three days. Wherever you looked, all you could see were hundreds, perhaps thousands of Daliesque breast-shaped dunes. For the first and last time since leaving Chegga I felt erotic.

The dunes were dark and heavy on the hard side, and marked by lines of diminutive ripples caused by the action of the wind. On the soft side they were lighter. The sand skimmed the surface, blown around the dunes' curves by the action of the wind. It is this subtle blending of dark and light in the dunes' curves that gives them their sensual beauty.

But in spite of the beauty it was hard going. The dunes reached heights of over six hundred feet, and seemed to stretch beyond eternity.

René Caillié had travelled in these same dunes on his way home from Timbuktu.

The poor animals moved with such difficulty that our progress was slow and painful; we advance but a mile an hour. . . .

Sidi-Aly, whom I questioned on the subject, and who at times vouchsafed an answer, assured me that in none of his previous travels in the Soudan had he seen such lofty sand-hills.[11]

For three days we trudged up and down those sand-hills. Sometimes the days defied reality, and I saw in those strange and fantastic shapes of sand the faces of John Davidson and the Sous-Préfet of Tindouf looking at me. Davidson's face was ghostly English, but on the Sous-Préfet's face was something different. It was the smile of a Cheshire Cat, a shadow of the shadow of a smile; a smile that knew more than I knew, understood more than I understood, the same smile that I had seen in Tindouf, a smile that was to oppress me all the way to the Soudan.

As I trudged on through the dunes, obsessed by that smile, my mind began to wander and my body wandered with my mind. Often I found myself leaving the caravan track without realizing it.

'Concentrate, *Nasrani*, concentrate,' Omar would shout when he saw me going off like that.

Dermas, on the other hand, was softer.

'This is the road to Taoudenni,' he would say, pointing to the right track. 'That is the road to Hell,' he added, pointing in the direction of my wanderings.

The Half-Child was neither soft nor hard. He just giggled at the antics of a grown-up from a different world.

Once Omar himself was dreaming. He had sent the Half-Child up a dune ahead of us to spy out the land, and was leading the camels himself, when a load slipped. The camel whose load had slipped was half-way down the caravan. I was at the front with Omar, and Dermas was at the back. There was no one in the middle. The camel panicked and reared into the air, plunging down the dune, taking the two camels tied to either end of him down with him. Dermas raced forward, but he was too late. I ran back, but by the time I arrived the three camels had disappeared down the side of the dune. Omar was just mumbling verses of the Koran to himself. By the time he heard Dermas's shout it had all happened long ago. Dermas and myself went down the sand

[11] Caillié, *op. cit.*, Vol. II.

slope to investigate. No camels' bones had broken. But there was something worse. One of the camels was carrying two of our waterskins. The camel had rolled over, bursting them both. They were lying open and almost empty on two damp patches in the sand.

We looked at each other in silence, then dug the camels out and continued.

Often as we laboured through those dunes I could hear strange rumblings, like the rolling of drums. Dermas, in all seriousness, told me that this was the laughter of Rul, the djinn of the dunes, who torments the traveller as he becomes disorientated by fear and thirst.

Omar gave off a guffaw. He knew perfectly well that it was nothing but the noise of the sand rolling down the dune in tiny avalanches created by our footsteps in the soft sand.

We came out of the dunes on the first of December. 'From here it is a flat plain all the way to Taghaza,' said Omar. I knew that Taoudenni was supposedly only four days away from Taghaza, and I could not resist the impulse to ask Omar how many days we were from Taghaza.

'Perhaps four, perhaps six, perhaps eight. *Inshallah.*' *Inshallah* was the only security that he had.

We were marching over a flat plain of sand and gravel. It was bare and bleak, with the wind roaring across it at gale force. We wrapped our howlis around our faces to protect them from the blasts of wind, and dragged our stubborn and reluctant camels behind us.

It was now eight days since we had left Bouir Ikrief. We had used up the last of our flour, I had run out of the tobacco that 'Mood had given me, and our water was getting low. Two water-skins had already been drunk, two others had been lost, and the remaining two were hanging limp and loose from Omar's white bull. Each was about three-quarters full.

Omar carefully inspected the two skins with water in them. He announced that it was too late to turn back to Bouir Ikrief. If we were to get to Taoudenni, we would have to limit ourselves to the absolute minimum of water. From now on, sand, not water, was to be used for washing our hands before and after we ate. The *nasrani*, especially, was to economize on water; he could no longer indulge in such wasteful habits as washing his teeth. What water we had was rationed to six glasses of tea per day for each person, and the same amount again, mixed with wheat and sugar, to give us strength. The only other water that we were to have was the water used for cooking.

Oh, those dry days, marching across that severe and forbidding plain. They were monotonous and never-ending and I was bored to the point of pain.

Increasingly I found that I was going on two journeys. One was a conscious journey, a physical one, from Tindouf, through Taoudenni, to Timbuktu. The other was an unconscious journey, 'an inner journey', you might say, that took me back into my own past, through a series of day-dreams and night-dreams, into the world of my own beginning, a world that I had long since forgotten.

'Beware, *Nasrani*,' Dermas said to me on the second day we were walking over the plain, as I day-dreamed. 'You will be attacked by djinns unless your mind gets stronger.'

'The demon of the noon-tide,' I thought.

Djinns are spirits, neither human nor divine, created out of fire and easily aroused. 'We have brought man into being from dry ringing clay which was wrought from black mud,' writes the Koran, 'and the Jinn we have brought into being before from the fire of the glowing blast.'[12]

In modern psychological terms the djinn is our own subconscious: a fire that is easily aroused and able to take on the shape of our fears. Just as Mohammed The Prophet confronted, converted, and thus overcame them, so we must confront our own djinns, recognize them, and thus transcend them.

I was ignorant of this at the time and so, with all the racial resources of the British stiff upper lip, I tried to avoid my djinns. But they followed me across the Sahara, mocking my attempts to pretend they were not there, haunting me with my fears and my past until, on the edge of the Soudan, I faced them, and thus destroyed them.

On the third day across the dunes the wind, which the Arabs

[12] *The Koran*, 15:28, trans. M. Z. Khan.

call the *Alizes*, was at its worst. It came at us behind our left shoulders, blowing long streamers of sand across the gravel. They slashed at our legs like vicious serpents. Dermas called these streamers 'Dancing Djinns', and indeed they had a ghostly and tormenting look to them. It was a terrible day. I wanted to lie down in the gravel, curl up with my back to the wind, and give up. But I knew I couldn't. If I so much as sat down on the ground, Omar would dismount from his camel and kick me as if I was some collapsed camel. So I plodded on, with *Mr Wilson* behind me, unable even to die in peace. As I took each resentful step forward, I cursed Omar for taking me through this dry wasteland, I cursed Allah for having only half created it, and I cursed myself for trying to cross it.

The flat plain seemed endless. The camels, who had had no grazing for two days, were regularly collapsing. The camels at the back of the caravan were lucky; they had Dermas, who would gently coax them onto their feet, whispering into their ears and unloading their baggage to help get them onto their feet. But the camels at the front were unlucky. They had Omar, who would dismount from his camel with a curse, kick or beat the victim to its feet, and then imperiously call Dermas forward to act as a mounting-block. Dermas was the only thing that got him onto his camel. He tried using me once, but I collapsed under his weight.

Then, half-way through the afternoon of the third day, the plain seemed to close in around us. Two great volcanic chains were pushing us into a bottleneck that went due south. At the entrance of the bottleneck there was a great table mountain. It looked ageless and impregnable, dominating the plain as it had once dominated the history of the Sahara. Throughout the Middle Ages it had been the cornerstone of the North African economy. Now it was nothing, except a great monument that stood out on the plain, defying the battering winds as it had once defied armies and nations.

'Taghaza,' Omar shouted above the roar of the wind. 'Four days from now Taoudenni, *Inshallah*.'

For five hundred years Taghaza had been the principal source of salt in the Sahara. Salt from Taghaza was sold in Timbuktu for equal weight of gold. During those years, Taghaza, unaffected by desert politics because of its natural defences, had gained great economic power. Its fame spread so far that it was mentioned on the Catalan Map of Charles V.

The Arab traveller, Ibn Battuta, gives the earliest first-hand account of the mines, in the fourteenth century.

[Taghaza was] an unattractive village, with the curious feature that its houses and Mosques are built of salt, roofed with camel skins. There are no trees there, nothing but sand. In the sand is the salt mine; they dig the salt, and find it in thick slabs. . . . No one lives at Taghaza except the slaves of the Mesufa tribe, who dig for the salt; they subsist on dates imported from Dra's and Sijilmasa, camel's flesh, and millet imported from the Negro lands. The negroes come up from their country and take away the salt from there. At Walata a load of salt brings eight to ten mithgals, in the town of Mali it sells for twenty to thirty, and sometimes as much as forty. The negroes use salt as a medium of exchange, just as gold and silver is used (elsewhere); they cut it up into pieces and buy and sell with it. The business done at Taghaza, for all its meanness, amounts to an enormous figure in terms of hundredweights of gold-dust.[13]

Two hundred years later another traveller, Leo Africanus, was to visit Taghaza on his way to the Soudan.

In this region is great store of salt digged, being whiter than any marble. This salt is taken out of certain caves and pits, at the entrance whereof stand their cottages, that work in the salt-mines. And as these workmen are all strangers, who sell the salt that they dig unto certain merchants that carry the same upon camels to the kingdom of Timbuktu, where there would otherwise be extreme scarcity of salt. Neither have the said diggers of salt any victuals but such as the merchants bring unto them; for they are distant from all inhabited places almost twenty days' journey, insomuch that oftentimes they perish for lack of food, whenas the merchants come not in due time unto them. Moreover, the south-east wind doth so often

[13] Battuta, *op. cit.*

blind them, that they cannot live here without great peril. I myself continued three days amongst them, all which time I was constrained to drink salt-water drawn from certain wells not far from the salt-pits.[14]

Leo's is the last description that we have of Taghaza as a working mine. A few years after his visit, the Sultan of Morocco, al-Mansur, sent an army down the Taghaza Road to occupy the mines. He hoped that by controlling the salt trade he would be able to control the gold trade. The Moroccan army arrived in 1556, but when they got to the mines, they found that most of the inhabitants had fled. The Songhai governor and those miners who had been unlucky enough not to have left in time, were quickly put to death. None of the other miners ever came back.

The Moroccans, unable to find labour to exploit the mines, were forced to close them down. Taghaza never reopened. The miners who had fled had found another salt deposit. Not only did it have the advantage of being a hundred and twenty miles closer to Timbuktu, but it was far larger than the salt deposit at Taghaza, and it had never been exploited. The Saharan nomads called it 'Taghaza al-Ghizlan'. But the miners gave it another name. They called it Taoudenni.

We camped that night in the bottleneck at the end of the plain of Taghaza. All around were blackened stones and broken calabashes. It was strange to see so many traces of man and yet to see no one. Taghaza was marked on my Michelin tourist map with three spots, to denote a historic monument. For the first time since crossing the frontier I had a clear idea where we were.

'Four more days to Taoudenni,' I wrote in my journal the next morning. We broke camp and began the march through the bottleneck. A screaming wind flung serpents of sand at our bare legs. By mid-morning my body was showing signs of fatigue; there was a general listlessness everywhere inside me, a constant nagging desire to go just a little slower. Omar's strict water rationing was wearing inroads into my body as well as my morale. My lips were cracked and bloody, and my throat tormented me

[14] Africanus, op. cit., Vol. III.

every time I tried to swallow the thick saliva that collected in my mouth. Only four more days to go.

The others were weakening too. Omar spent most of the time travelling on top of the white bull, complaining that he was too ill to walk. He sat up there moaning away at the pain in his stomach, complaining to Allah at the injustices that he was suffering. The Half-Child, too, was in a miserable state. Throughout the day this little triumph of the human species walked on in his bare feet without complaining. But at night he would cry himself to sleep. Only Dermas went on as if all was normal. His feet were beginning to drag and his lips had turned grey, but he out-did everyone in sheer hard work.

It was Dermas who was really keeping the caravan together. This voluntary slave, this collaborating victim of economic exploitation, was taking on all the responsibilities of the caravan single-handed. While the rest of us sulked in the background, obsessed by our own private complaints, Dermas loaded the camels, unloaded them, searched for firewood, built the fire, slept with the camels at night and watched over them as they grazed in the morning.

The camels were in a far worse state than we were. It was over ten days since they had drunk water, and in the last five days they had only had grazing twice. They were walking more slowly than usual, they rarely roared now, but they were constantly flopping down onto the ground in a collapse. Even Omar's white bull was beginning to stumble, like a drunken giant trying to look sober. *Mr Wilson*, perhaps because he did not have the weight of my body on him much, seemed stronger than the rest. He was resilient and reliable, even though a little slow. He had been named well.

Walking on towards Taoudenni I felt helplessly and hopelessly crushed. Often I would escape from these depressions into the utterly trivial: the words of a pop song, the details of a television advertisement, the lines of a poem. But always the diversions ended by bringing me back to water.

                              If there were water
            And no rock

If there were rock
And also water
And water
A spring
A pool among the rock ...
But there is no water[15]

We moved out of the bottleneck of Taghaza onto a sea bed of sand and rock. Beyond was a grey plateau. We climbed onto it and found ourselves standing on a table formed by layers of flat and grey stone slabs. We stayed on those slabs all day, carefully guiding the camels so that their feet would not get caught in the crevices between the slabs. At the end of the table was a range of sand-dunes. It was evening. Instead of stopping, Omar led us off to the west.

'I know this place,' he said, pointing to a depression just beyond the range. 'Over there, there is grazing.'

It was pitch black by the time we reached the end of the dunes. Omar led us down into the depression, and after studying the ground he told us to make camp.

It was a moonless night. We slowly sipped our ration of water mixed with sugar and wheat, then we made tea. Instead of knocking it back, as nomads usually do, Omar and Dermas sipped it appreciatively, as if it was the last glass of tea they would ever have. As we drank our tea, Omar cooked the usual monotonous meal of rice and dried camel meat. We ate the meal in silence. Then we slept.

That night I had a dream about the *Titanic*. I was a steerage passenger on the liner. I had washed my face and pulled the plug out of the wash basin. The sea water came up through the plughole and the ship began to sink.

I awoke next morning to the call to pray. It filled the desert air as if it was the only sound in the world. I had woken from a dream into another dream.

'Three more days to Taoudenni,' I wrote in my journal. Three more days of cold starts, aching legs, dried lips, and swollen

[15] T. S. Eliot, *The Waste Land*, London, 1922.

throat. Three more days of awful agonizing monotony. Three more days.

Sometime that day, I estimated, we would be crossing the Tropic of Cancer. What a supremely unimportant piece of information that seemed.

At midday Omar took us off the route. He told me he wanted to check a water-hole. 'It is only a couple of kilometres away,' he said cheerfully.

I had already learnt to distrust a nomad's sense of distance, but I still innocently believed that there must be some connection between distances stated and distances meant. So I walked on, elated at the idea that soon, God willing, we would have unlimited supplies of water. Of course Omar had never mentioned this water-hole before, and Dermas had shrugged his shoulders when Omar spoke of it, but it was water all the same.

We passed up and down different layers of rock. On every new horizon I strained my eyes in search of Omar's water-hole, but it never came. An hour passed. A second hour passed. I was exasperated; we had been walking for miles.

'Calm down, *Nasrani*. Steady, steady,' said Omar good-naturedly.

This was too much to take. I turned on Omar in anger. I told him that he had no business stating distances that were so far apart from reality.

He was silent, shocked at my sudden assertion of myself. For a moment he feared a rebellion. Then the expression on his face changed.

'All right, *Nasrani*. Steady,' his mouth said. But his eyes said something else: 'Watch out, *Nasrani*, watch out,' they seemed to say.

We trudged on in silence, my mind wandering into liquid day-dreams.

'If there were the sound of water only.'[16]

Finally we arrived at Omar's water-hole. It was marked by a pile of slates. Close by three camels, their swollen stomachs filled with drifting sand, lay at rest.

The Half-Child ran over and removed the slates. He threw off

[16] T. S. Eliot, *op. cit.*

his kimono and climbed down into the black hole, wearing only his white sports pants. He splashed around for a while, and then he emerged with a wooden calabash half filled with water.

He handed it to Omar. Omar told him to give it to me.

'You first, *Nasrani*, since you were so concerned that we should get to the water.'

I uttered a sincere '*Bismellah*' and took up the bowl. Those were the first words that Omar had spoken to me since my outburst of anger nearly an hour before. I could feel the cool edge of the calabash on my swollen lips. I moved my lips around the brim appreciatively, and opened my mouth. As I gulped the water down I doubled up in a violent fit of coughing and nausea. It was salt water.

There was a grin of satisfaction on Omar's face. Dermas had turned away, wanting no part in Omar's tricks. The Half-Child was mimicking me and giggling with delight.

Once again the *nasrani* had been put firmly in his place.

The sky was silent now. The wind was asleep, and the two black buzzards who had been following us from Chegga had flown away. I thought of Taoudenni. 'Industrial hell . . .', 'even under the most merciless regime . . .', '. . . legendary hell-hole . . .'. I could hardly blame them leaving us.

'Two more days and we will be at Taoudenni,' I finally said to Omar, making my peace.

'Oh no, *Nasrani*. The camels have been travelling very slowly. It will be another three days before we reach Taoudenni.'

'Three more days to Taoudenni.' We spent the next day travelling over stretches of green shingle. On one side of us was an escarpment, the shingle stacked up against it. Thin lines of white rock, running parallel to the cliff, gave the impression of breaking waves, and the green shingle looked like a northern sea. It was a neurotic and petrifying landscape, which mocked at my thirst and threatened my sense of reality.

Constantly I would retreat into the utterly trivial. 'One hundred paces a minute . . . That's 6,000 paces an hour . . . About 36,000 paces each day.' By the time I reached Timbuktu, I calculated, I would have walked nearly two million paces. It was hardly a cheerful calculation. I had not yet walked a million, but already I was ready to give up.

'Two more days to Taoudenni,' I put in my journal. 'That's 72,000 steps.' The previous night Omar had found the camels a little grazing. They were travelling better today, but still they slipped and stumbled. Only the white bull had the strength to roar; the others just stared resignedly in their pointless and stubborn way.

I looked at the two waterskins which Omar's white bull was carrying. There was no more than three pints in each. I remember reading before I left England of a European's minimum water requirements each day. Six pints were recommended, and without those six pints you would dry up in less than twenty-four hours. There was one consolation, however. Death by thirst is supposed to be painless. According to those who were lucky enough to have survived, you retreat from reality into a peaceful 'high', and do not feel a thing.

I found the idea of being so close to death a little depressing. There were still so many things I wanted to do. Up until then I had always seen myself as the 'B' movie hero. Others might die, but not me. Now I realized that the end could be very soon. The normal practice in the desert of sending a man on a camel ahead to find water and bring it back, was out of the question. Not even Omar's white bull was capable of a gallop to Taoudenni and back within twenty-four hours.

Of course we didn't die. Nothing as dramatic as that happened. My main memories of that day are of boredom and indifference. I put my feet forward, one after the other, mechanically and out of habit. Life on the edge of death, I discovered to my disappointment, can be just as mundane as life anywhere else.

Looking back on that day, it is strange to recall that Taoudenni, that 'legendary hell-hole', became my ideal place. Life might be degraded there, but it was life all the same. Walking through that perilous but extremely boring day, Taoudenni grew in my estimation into some sort of wonderful place, an oasis of humanity. My Shangri La.

We camped that night on a patch of grass. The last grazing

that there was before Taoudenni. While the Half-Child collected fuel for the fire, Dermas and myself cut down bundles of grass to take with us to Taoudenni for the camels. Taoudenni, being a salt-pan, was incapable of natural life. After we had eaten, we prepared ourselves for our arrival at Taoudenni. Omar mixed some green powder with a little of the salt water that he had brought with him and hennaed his fingers. Dermas took up Omar's broken mirror and trimmed his beard with a pair of scissors. The Half-Child sat in silence, waiting for Omar to finish his fingers, so Omar could shave the Half-Child's head.

When Dermas had finished trimming his beard, I took up the mirror and studied my face. I looked like a walking giblet. A month's growth of beard did not hide a drawn face, a dripping nose, lacerated lips, and a black tongue. My hair was dry and tangled, my teeth were almost green, and my face was covered in sores. My clothes were filthy and stained with camel pee, and my breath must have smelt revolting.

That night I destroyed all compromising documents: notes on Mali's political background, copies of United Nations declarations on forced labour and slavery, a pamphlet published by the Anti-Slavery Association, and two press-cards. Then, with Dermas's scissors, I cut out all dangerous references to Taoudenni in my journal.

We left the next morning with a feeling of repressed excitement. The longer you spend trying to get somewhere, the more astonished you are when you realize you are about to get there. I no longer feared Taoudenni. It had become some marvellous place where we had mortgaged our lives, and now we were going to pay off that mortgage. I had completely forgotten about the American, the Frenchman, and the German. It didn't matter that there was no water left. It didn't matter if all the camels flopped down and never got up. All that mattered was that we were within walking distance of Taoudenni. We had reached the perimeter of safety. We were less than one day away from Shangri La.

It will be a long time before I forget that last day coming into Taoudenni. We marched over stretches of green shingle, swung south onto a great expanse of gravel, and climbed an escarpment onto a carpet of brilliantly-coloured pebbles. From the carpet of pebbles we descended onto a plain of sand and stones, which stretched out in front of us like a mushroom omelette. We crossed the plain, and came to a range of mountains made of black and purple slabs of stone. Omar led us to a pass which took us through these Dantesque mountains and at the top of the pass he motioned to the caravan to halt.

Below us lay a desolate and bare pan of salt, shining white in the sun. It stretched for about ten square miles, hemmed in by buttes of sandstone and table mountains. Right out of the centre of the salt-pan loomed a huge table mountain, more monumental than the others, more imposing.

'Taoudenni,' said Omar.

The gates to Hell could not have looked bleaker.

5

The Slaves of Taoudenni

Abandon Hope all ye who enter here
Dante, *Inferno*

Tahar Omar led the way down the mountain pass onto the salt pan below. As we walked across the pan, stubbing our toes on the hard, jagged crust of salt, I could distinguish a clutter of buildings standing alone amidst the flat and barren desolation. It was a late, colourless afternoon. The sun had slipped down beyond the table mountain, casting the whole area in shadow. Around the buildings I could see tiny specks of humanity moving around like ants.

'The place of water,' Omar growled with a hoarse voice that suggested a horribly dry throat. 'And over there,' he said, pointing to beyond the table mountain, 'the place of salt.'

Since his earliest days man has needed sodium chloride, common salt. His earliest settlements were always near salt-licks, formed a hundred and fifty million years ago, when a series of droughts dried up hundreds of rivers and lakes throughout Africa and Asia. Salt, like water, is essential to man. In order to live, man needs three and a half ounces of salt in his body at all times. Without it he will suffer withdrawal symptoms, degenerate, and ultimately perish.

Primitive man maintained this level of salt by eating raw meat. But once he began to boil and stew his food, he removed the salt from it. Man had to pay for this culinary refinement by setting out in search of salt. Tribal wars were fought over salt licks. Those tribes who had sufficient salt flourished, and those without it declined.

Three exceptions prove the rule. Homer, in the *Odyssey*, wrote with amazement of tribes in the interior of Asia Minor who survived without salt. Sallust, in the first century B.C., recorded that the Numidians never ate salt. Today the bedouins of Hadhramaut in Saudi Arabia exist without salt. All three groups, however, ate roast meat and drunk large quantities of milk, which provided them with the necessary amount.

When man evolved from a hunter into a farmer, his need for salt became more acute. The cereal crops that he cultivated contained no salt at all. Salt became so important that it ranked in stature with fire and water. Not only was it essential for survival, but it had in it unique preservative qualities. Meat and corpses caked in salt could be kept for long periods of time.

And so, to the gods that men worshipped, suitable offerings were made, bread and salt. The Old Testament tells how Moses commanded the Children of Israel to sprinkle salt on the meat that they offered to Jehovah.

It had secular symbolism, too. Salt represented health, friendship, and virtue. Newly-born babies were rubbed in it to give them long life. Guests were offered bread and salt as symbols of friendship. The Persian expression *namak haram*, untrue to salt, meant disloyalty and treachery.

With the advent of trade, salt began to be used as a medium of exchange and a source of taxation. The Roman legionaries were paid in salt; the word salary is derived from the Latin *salarium*, which means salt money. As long ago as 2197 B.C., the Chinese Emperor Lu imposed a tax on salt. In nineteenth-century Italy the high tax on salt provoked the riots of May Day 1898. In the 1930s and '40s Gandhi used the tax on salt, originally imposed by the East India Company, as a catalyst to launch his Indian independence movement, urging his followers to flout authority by collecting salt from the sea.

Salt had other uses, too. Pompey discovered an antidote against poison, 'to be taken fasting, and a grain of salt to be added'. Petronius, in the *Satyricon*, coined the expression 'not worth his salt', and Cicero, writing about friendship, warns: 'Trust no man until you have eaten much salt with him'.

We marched on. As we got closer, the buildings began to define themselves. There were three forts, each one representing a different era in the history of the Sahara. The oldest of these, to the left, was sixteenth-century, built in the days of the Songhai Empire, following the abandoning of the mines at Taghaza. Now it was no more than a ruin. Its corner towers had fallen down, its ramparts had crumbled, and its windward side was piled high with sand that sloped down to a graveyard close by.

The middle fort, the only one that was inhabited, was of standard French colonial style, very Beau Geste. From its high watchtower a grubby Malian flag flapped upside down in the wind. Outside the main gate were two sandbagged dugouts. Ugly reels of barbed wire protected the approaches to the fort like starving concertinas.

To the right of the barbed wire was the third fort, a low-lying concrete blockhouse, totalitarian style. It was only half-built but already seedy, with human excrement littered around it and garbage piled high against one side.

Between the French colonial fort and the modern concrete blockhouse stood 'the place of water'. From the high watchtower of the middle fort a heavy machine-gun poked its muzzle down at the water-hole. It gave one a persecution complex just to look at it.

I followed Omar towards the water-hole. As we rounded the concrete blockhouse we came upon a white Land-Rover with large Red Cross markings on it. A line of Russian half-tracks, stripped of their wheels, tyres, tracks, guns and seats, lay limp and useless beside it, as dead as the camel carcasses that we had seen on our way to Taoudenni.

I felt uneasy walking across that crust of salt towards the middle fort, and I felt uneasier still, when a posse of soldiers came out to greet us. They were led by a sergeant wearing plastic sandals and carrying a rifle by its middle. When he recognized me as a *nasrani*, he hoisted his rifle up to a firing position with alarming alacrity and ordered me to halt. The soldiers surrounded me and stared. I stood there on the salt-pan, surrounded by curious soldiers, feeling a little scared and very stupid, while the sergeant dispatched a corporal, who wore nothing but a stained combat jacket and a pair of dirty underpants, to fetch the Commandant.

He ran off, while the group of soldiers guarding me stared in silence. A couple of minutes later, the Corporal emerged from the fort with a pair of officers and a pair of trousers. The leading officer was a Moor. He was tall and fair-skinned, and wore an army greatcoat and a khaki turban, which he was winding tightly round his face to protect it from the wind. Behind him his adjutant, a short black man in a natty, well-cut uniform, flashed white teeth and sunglasses.

'The Commandant is an Arab,' Omar whispered to me, boosting my confidence. 'He is a good friend of mine.'

Tahar Omar and the Commandant greeted each other in traditional nomad style. Only after the ancient greeting had run through its course, did the Commandant ask Omar to explain my presence. The two men spoke quietly in Arabic.

After a while I saw them laugh. I could hear Omar mimicking me. Then the Commandant turned to greet me. His house was my house, he said, as the Moslem cliché goes. He asked me if I had had a good journey, and told me that he would personally find me a caravan to take me on to Timbuktu, 'at the earliest possible opportunity,' he added. I didn't like that bit.

'Is there anything else that you want?' he asked me. There was no doubt, he was a most charming man.

'Yes,' I replied. 'I want some water.'

The Commandant and his adjutant led us to the nearby well. It was an ugly, mean-looking affair, made of wire and scaffolding. A normal sight in the Sahara, but with one exception: instead of having camels attached to the ropes to pull up the water, there were two men in harnesses; Tuaregs, they wore nothing but rags. The two Tuaregs stared at me in dumb amazement. Who were they? What had they done? Why were they victims of such outrageous behaviour? I don't know. To me they looked more like two-legged animals than men; beasts of burden, their humanity withered away and their feelings reduced to mere sensations . . . and yet they were human beings, they *must* have been human beings, with all the hope and promise that that implies.

(And God created men 'vice-regents of the earth' says the Koran.)

I gave Omar a glance that begged for moral support. He returned it with a look of disapproval. 'This is how the world is, *Nasrani*,' that look seemed to say. 'And neither you nor I can do anything that will ever change it.'

We stopped at the well only a couple of feet away from them. The Adjutant gave a parade-ground shout and the two beasts of burden started walking ahead, erect and slow as they pulled their ropes behind them. As they took each step forward mechanically, their eyes stared stonily ahead in death-like indifference. They walked about a hundred and fifty yards, and then stopped automatically. Two leather buckets had emerged from the black hole, twisting and turning on the taut ropes, and spilling their water as they swung round. The Commandant leaned over the well and grabbed one of the buckets. He poured the water into a wooden bowl and handed it to me.

'*Bismellah*,' he said. 'In the name of God.'

I took up the bowl. The hydrogen sulphide in the water gave off a stench of bad eggs. It smelt foul and it tasted foul. But I was thirsty. I gulped it down greedily, as spasms of pain shot up from my dried-up throat. It was only after I drank it that I recalled a passage from Sadi's history, the *Tarik es-Sudan*. When an army passed through Taoudenni in 1652, 'the water, attacking the men's intestines, caused dysentery and killed many of them'.

After the four of us had drunk our fill, the Commandant led us to a small hut close by the fort. Here we could camp for the night, he said; expressly, but politely, forbidding me from entering the fort.

We settled the camels on their haunches and begun to unload them. While I was working, the Adjutant explained, in his clipped West African French, how lucky I was to be going to Timbuktu.

'It is civilization,' he said with a touch of envy. 'There are cafés, bars, whisky and women.' His pimp-like eyes gloated on the details. 'Black women, brown women and even fair-skinned women, and very cheap. Sometimes you do not even have to pay.'

He was used to civilization, he told me. Here at Taoudenni he missed the gay cosmopolitan life. With my ignorance of Timbuktu, I took his words at their face value. At the time I did not know that there was only one café and two bars, that the whisky was in short supply, reserved almost exclusively for the military, and that the brothel was a sand-dune behind the Post Office.

He rambled on without offering help. I felt a moral superiority bordering on arrogance; sex was the last thing on my mind. But I could not bring myself to ask him to shut up. When your breath smells revolting, and your clothes are stained with camel pee, you feel at a social disadvantage confronting a man flashing white teeth and sunglasses.

He gave me a voyeur's grin and offered me a cigarette. It came from a packet with the trade-name *Liberté* stamped across it. I accepted it and smiled in gratitude. Misunderstanding it, he returned my smile with an even broader grin. It had no meaning. It was promiscuous, loveless, and only skin-deep.

When the unloading was over, the meticulous inspection of our baggage began. The soldiers threw themselves into the task with relish, more like booty-hunters than upholders of law and order. My money was carefully examined, my camera and films were confiscated, and I was asked if I had a radio.

After I had been thoroughly searched and inadequately interrogated, the Adjutant began to write the details of my passport in a school exercise book, the garrison log. He wrote laboriously with large childish handwriting. Half-way through, he broke his pencil. I offered him a ball-point pen. The Adjutant looked at me suspiciously, then asked if I would give it to him.

When the Commandant and his adjutant had finished their interrogation, they returned to their role as hosts. They were charming and generous to me. They walked back to the fort and returned with a leg of camel meat for Omar, and a couple of packets of cigarettes for me. As well as the cigarettes, the Adjutant brought a file of pornographic photographs. What he wanted, he told me with sincerity, was an honest European's view of these treasures. He handled them with pride, carefully undoing the string that was tied round so as not to bend them. He treated them like some old family heirloom. It was understandable; they were all that he had to remind him of the gay cosmopolitan life. I thumbed through them with disinterest. Taoudenni was hardly the place to have erotic thoughts. The Half-Child peered over my shoulder with wonder and amazement. Dermas looked on with amused tolerance. Omar gave a harsh grunt of god-fearing disapproval, and the Commandant did his best to look the other way.

And then something happened; something sudden and unexpected that neither the Commandant, the Adjutant, nor myself could have foreseen. As I turned over a page to see a slightly yellowed and over-exposed picture of a middle-aged Moroccan lady with her legs open wide to display that great mystery of creation, the Sergeant who had originally called on me to halt, ran up to the Commandant and, clicking his plastic sandals to attention, announced in French:

'A prisoner has escaped.'

'Speak in Arabic,' the Commandant told him quietly.

I did not understand the conversation that followed; it was as if a door had been closed on me. The Commandant and the Sergeant were talking in whispers. It ended with the Commandant making his apologies to me and marching off with the Sergeant to the fort. The Adjutant quickly gathered up his pictures, tied them together with string, and ran off after them. They disappeared into the fort and emerged a few minutes later with a nomad scout and half a dozen soldiers. They marched off at the double to the Red Cross Land-Rover, the only vehicle in Taoudenni that worked. When the Commandant, the Adjutant and the scout had climbed into the front and the soldiers had piled into the back, the Land-Rover crunched into gear and roared off into the night.

So Taoudenni did have something to hide—and I had taken it by surprise.

The next morning I was not awoken by Omar's call to prayer. I was abruptly shocked into consciousness by the sound of 'Reveille' on a bugle. I was not allowed to wander around and I was not so unwise as to write my journal in public, so I spent the morning 'hanging around', waiting for the afternoon, when we were to march the last four miles of our journey to the salt-mines of Taoudenni.

While sitting around the fire, a young nomad came up to us.

'My son,' Omar announced, introducing him to me. 'He has been in Taoudenni all summer.'

Sayed ben (son of) Omar was the most sophisticated nomad that I met on the journey. It is significant that he never called me a *nasrani*; he was the only nomad who called me by my name. He had been educated in Tindouf, could speak French fluently, and had an easy confident air about him. It was soon apparent that he had an awareness of the world that stretched far beyond the frontiers of the Sahara. All his life he had been in contact with the radio.

Though he was sophisticated and civilized, he had not lost that toughness and love of freedom that is so vital to the nomad. He had made the journey across the Tanezrouft from Timbuktu to Taoudenni in late May and early June, the hottest time of the year. René Caillié had made his journey at the same time and had nearly died, but to Sayed ben Omar it had been perfectly normal.

While we were drinking tea, I asked him if he would exchange his life in the desert for an easier existence in a town.

'No, I prefer the nomad life, the freedom,' he said in that vague, all-embracing way that is so typical of the Saharaui.

While we were drinking tea he saw in my baggage the Michelin map of north-west Africa. Unlike his father, he did not scorn maps. He politely asked if he could have a look at it, and studied it with fascination. As well as being able to identify places like Tindouf, Taoudenni and Timbuktu, he pointed out other places that he knew of only by hearsay—Bechar, Casablanca and Algiers. He asked me where Cairo was, and I told him that the map did not extend far enough to the east. So with his finger he drew a line in the sand, extending the North African coastline as far as the Sinai Desert, then up along the Levant to an elongated half-circle to mark Turkey.

'Is that right?' he asked. I complimented him on his wide geographical knowledge. 'That is easy,' he said modestly, 'it is the details that require learning. The man who made this map must have been a very intelligent person.'

I never made that short journey to the salt-mines by camel. Instead the Commandant and his adjutant offered me a lift there in the Red Cross Land-Rover. It was an offer that I could not have refused.

The Land-Rover bumped across the flat and scarred salt crust, quickly overtaking Omar's tiny caravan which, for thirty days, had been my entire world. On our way we passed the ruins of several previous Taoudennis, left as ghost towns after the salt around them had been fully exploited. Now I understood why no two maps marked Taoudenni on the same spot. It was constantly moving around the salt pan. In the last forty years, Omar told me, there had been three different Taoudennis.

We drove for a quarter of an hour over a bare landscape of salt, until we finally came within sight of the mines of Taoudenni. They were a jumble of shallow trenches, about three feet deep, stretched over several acres. Inside these trenches the miners worked in pairs, one hacking out the salt and the other baling out water. The miners were both Negroes and Arabs. I was astonished that here in the middle of the Sahara the salt mines should be in danger of flooding. Later the Commandant told me that the salt underneath Taoudenni was impermeable. The water collected below the layers of salt, building up great pressure. As the thin crust of salt was broken, so the water gushed out at great force.

Close to these open mines was a transit area. Here the blocks of salt were stacked up, ready to be loaded onto the camels that would carry them down to Timbuktu. The area was littered with camel dung.

Spread out around the transit area, moving towards the centre in an ever-decreasing circle, was what appeared to be a work-party, collecting up the dung for fuel. The party was under the supervision of two soldiers, who stood around chatting, looking bored and disinterested. When the soldiers saw the Land-Rover approach, they suddenly began running around in a flurry of activity, urging their prisoners with the butts of their rifles to work faster. The Land-Rover stopped, and the Commandant leaned out of the window to speak to them. While the attention of the two soldiers was diverted, the party of prisoners stopped their work and focused their hopeless and reproaching eyes on me. Why me? Perhaps because I was a *nasrani*, they thought that I was to blame for all this? Maybe they saw in me some chance of

I

freedom? I don't know. Nor do I know how long they stared at me like that. It might have been five seconds, it might have been five minutes. Time means little in such circumstances. All I remember are those silent half-dead eyes, and the outburst of protest that hovered on my lips and died there, as the Land-Rover jerked into gear and drove off again.

It is horrible even to have to recall it all. I saw everything. Yet I comprehended nothing.

'You have a well-run establishment here,' I said sarcastically.

The Adjutant flashed a grin with his white teeth and sunglasses, as if to take me into his confidence.

'Progress,' he said, with that same religious finality with which Omar would say *Hamdullah*.

The town of Taoudenni itself was the meanest looking, most impoverished collection of dwellings that I have ever seen. It was made up of tiny hovels built out of blocks of salt and roofed with sheets of corrugated iron and flattened cardboard boxes. Flies buzzed everywhere, and human excrement decorated the surroundings without shame. It was shocking to think of human beings living there. Yet they did, two thousand of them, all males, producing three thousand tons of salt each year, in a manner no different from that described by Ibn Battuta six hundred years earlier.

Inside these hovels was no better than outside. The huts were dark and airless. Apart from the doors, made out of corrugated iron, there was no ventilation anywhere. What little light there was, came from thin shafts of sunlight that squeezed their way through the spaces between the salt blocks. The thought of disease oppressed me.

I was shown the hut that I was to stay in; it was more like a prison cell than a rest house. There I was introduced to the two soldiers who were detailed to 'look after me' (a polite and charming form of house arrest). While the two soldiers were eyeing me suspiciously, the Adjutant was offering me more information about Timbuktu.

I had to be very careful about disease, he said. Once he had been to Timbuktu on leave and had not taken the necessary precautions.

'There is no penicillin in Taoudenni,' he said, recalling the scene. 'It was very painful.'

The Commandant and the Adjutant left, and I fell asleep; not because I was tired, but because it was the only way that I could escape from the darkness and depression around me. I awoke in the evening to a gabble of voices. A collection of men had gathered outside my hut. The two soldiers were trying to shoo them away. But the voices were adamant. They would not go.

What did they want? I asked one of the soldiers. They wanted *dowa*, medicine, the soldier replied. Did I have any *dowa*? Yes, I did. The two soldiers consulted for a while in low murmurs. After a few moments they agreed that it would do no harm for the *nasrani* to share out his *dowa* with the sick. So they let the waiting men in, one at a time.

As well as the usual nomadic diseases of trachoma, rheumatism, and hypochondria, most suffered from acute dysentery and lacerated feet. Both complaints are caused by the hydrogen sulphide in the water, which eats into the internal systems and edges itself into the soles of the feet. There was little that I could do but feed them with anti-diarrhoea pills and rub penicillin ointment into their feet. Even simple prescriptions like that, however, caused rows. Those who were given pills demanded ointment, and those who were given ointment demanded pills.

I was halfway through my amateur surgery when there was a commotion outside. A group of miners had queue-barged the line of waiting patients. They were carrying between them a man lying on a sheet of corrugated iron. The two soldiers were barring their way, arguing with them furiously. They told the miners to go to the end of the queue, claiming that it was indecorous to jump in front. The miners claimed that they could not wait. The man was dying. Allah would not wait. The introduction of Allah into the argument decided the issue. Reluctantly the soldiers allowed the dying man in.

He was dying all right. That was clear. His eyes were dull, his cheeks were sunken, and he smelt of death—for there is such a smell. What was he dying of? Perhaps dysentery, perhaps overwork, perhaps just hopelessness. I tried to get him to point at the pain, but in no way could I register on his consciousness. As far as he was concerned, I did not exist; nor did the soldiers exist, nor the miners for that matter. Only Allah existed. He moaned away at his god, mumbling to himself verses of the Koran, praying for forgiveness and deliverance.

I tried to make some sense out of him, I really tried. His pulse beat and his lungs functioned in a gasping way, but he was totally beyond us mortals. Though he was still technically alive, he was already in another place. God knows where. There was nothing I could do, I told the onlookers, and I shrugged my shoulders in a hopeless, fatalistic way.

The miners saw my shrug and let out a jabber of protest. Even the two soldiers joined in. They were shocked at the *nasrani's* apparent disregard for human life. They imagined that I was refusing to bring him back to life on purpose.

I knew that there was nothing that I could do, but I also knew that I must be seen to do something. So I crushed two pain-killing tablets into a tiny bowl of water, and spoonfed him. The white muck dribbled out of the corners of his mouth onto his blanket. But the miners and soldiers were still not happy. They demanded more *dowa*, good *dowa*. I had no intention of wasting any more painkillers on a man already so far away, so I crushed two aspirins instead, spoonfeeding him again and watching the *dowa* dribble down onto the blanket again. None of it had gone into his mouth, but this time they were happy. They nodded and smiled with approval, and took him away; to die in peace, I hope.

I finished my surgery and escaped once again into the oblivion of sleep. I wasn't tired. It was pure escapism. I awoke in the middle of the night and smoked a cigarette. When I had finished the cigarette, I felt a sudden loosening in my bowels. The brackish waters of Taoudenni had done their dirty worst, and my innards —which until now had been remarkably stable—began to rumble and gurgle in drunken disorder. I rushed out into the night— once, twice, three times. The two guards outside made no objection. The reputation of *nasranis* for being weak in the bowels is widespread throughout Africa.

It was on these excursions into the night that I was able to meet and talk to the miners of Taoudenni. I found a group of them huddled around a camel-dung fire a couple of hovels away. From them I was able to get an idea of the monotony and the apathy of life in the mines, and to fill in the gaps in my knowledge about Taoudenni. They were slaves all right. They worked the mines under a system known as debt-bondage. They were either debtors who had been sent to Taoudenni to pay off their debts, or juvenile delinquents and petty criminals who had been 'advised' by the police to go there to avoid prosecution. They worked a seven-day week: five days for either the state or their creditors, the other two days for themselves, to pay for the tea, sugar, rice, and tobacco that men like Tahar Omar brought to the mines and sold at vastly inflated prices.

I asked if any of the miners had come to Taoudenni voluntarily. A few had, they said. They came during the famine, when there was no other work. They had all gone away now.

Did they work the salt-mines all year round? No. They worked from September until May. During the hot summer they were able to return to Timbuktu—at least the debtors were. The civil and political prisoners had to work all year round.

Political prisoners? I was interested. They shrugged their shoulders vaguely. There was little they could tell me. They were kept in a camp five kilometres away, beyond some sand dunes that they gestured to. Apart from those who drew water at the garrison, and those who collected camel dung for the soldiers' fuel, they were never seen. They had their own mines which the soldiers kept everyone well away from.

How many were there? One thousand, said one. Two thousand, said another. Ten thousand, said a third. No one really knew. One miner from Djenne told me that he had seen barge-loads of prisoners sail down the River Niger towards Timbuktu, where a transit camp had been built after the Malian army's coup d'état had overthrown the Marxist government in 1969.

So the political prisoners were Marxists? Not all of them, I was told. Some were capitalists who had originally been sent to prison by the Marxists. No one has ever bothered to release them. An ex-schoolteacher told me all this. He had been 'advised' to go to Taoudenni by the police. His only crime appeared to be that he had been educated.

And what about the Tuaregs, I asked him. There were many Tuaregs in the camp, he told me. The authorities seemed to prefer Tuareg to Negro prisoners. The Tuaregs came from the desert; they lived longer and worked better than the other miners.

I had heard about the fate of the Tuaregs before I left England. They had revolted against their black rulers and had been quickly crushed by the Malian army. The army used very effective tactics against these rebels. They made them dig pits of four cubic metres, and threw blazing embers into these pits. Then they threw the Tuaregs in. It was this mindless brutality that prompted the Russians to abandon Mali, abandoning it in the same way, and at the same time, as the Americans abandoned Haiti. The excesses in those two countries had become ideological liabilities.

And yet it is an ill-wind that does not blow some good. The most notable butcher of the war was a certain Malian army officer, Major Silas Diarra Dily. After the coup, he quarrelled with the 'Revolutionary Council'. He was quickly despatched to Taoudenni, where he had sent so many Tuareg. There—I record with a certain amount of satisfaction—he died.

I asked the schoolteacher if Taoudenni was the only camp for political prisoners.

'No, there is another at Kidal. The President and his immediate advisers are kept there. The less important political prisoners go to Taoudenni.'

There was one more question that I wanted to ask him. Had anything been heard of a prisoner who had escaped two nights previously? Yes, they had heard that a prisoner had escaped, but they knew no more. He had either been recaptured or he was dead.

'Is there any other possibility?'

'No, there is nowhere to go. No one has ever escaped from Taoudenni and lived.'

I returned to my hovel disgusted; disgusted by the suffering, the senselessness, the cruelty, and by the darkness, the utter darkness that hung over Taoudenni like a cloud, suffocating the emotions and dulling the sense of human solidarity. More than anything else, I wanted to escape from this evil place, to get away from the squalor, the smell, the disease, and the darkness.

The next morning I received another visit from the Commandant and his adjutant. The Commandant announced that he had found a caravan of salt that would take me to Timbuktu. It would leave the next morning. At that very moment the caravan master was on his way here to meet me and discuss the financial arrangements.

The caravan master came into the hovel while I was smoking one of the Adjutant's cigarettes. He stood to attention, knocked his head on the cardboard roof, clicked his bare feet together, and gave a ridiculous para-military salute. That salute was the first thing that I disliked about him.

After the traditional nomad greeting, the Commandant introduced this newcomer to me as 'Hotan of the Berebish tribe'. I did not catch his full name.

'Hotan of the Berebish tribe' was everything that Tahar Omar was not. While Omar was short, fat and sophisticated, Hotan was tall, thin and simple. Although about forty years old, he had the eyes of a child. His beard and closely-cropped hair were as blue as his clothes, and his finely-featured face had a lean and hungry look to it.

I had very little money, so on Omar's advice I arranged a deal with Hotan whereby I would swop my carthorse of a camel with a fresh one, and then give it to Hotan, in lieu of payment, when we reached Timbuktu. Hotan was happy and I was happy, so we accepted the arrangement without more ado. I noted with reservations that he was far more interested in the quantities of tea and sugar that I would be bringing with me, and in the letter of recommendation that he hoped I would write to the petroleum exploration team that was based in Timbuktu. In contrast with Omar, money didn't seem to interest Hotan.

When the negotiations were finished, the Commandant asked me if there were any further questions that I wanted to put to Hotan.

Yes, there was. Throughout my journey from Chegga I had continually felt isolated because of my inability to express anything but the most basic Arabic. Could Hotan speak French?

'Yes,' said Hotan, 'I can speak French a little,' but he said it in Arabic. That was the second thing that I disliked about him, his preference for telling me what he thought I wanted to hear, when all I wanted to hear was the truth.

'And are there any questions that Hotan wants to ask the *nasrani*?' the Commandant asked.

'Yes, there is. Does the *nasrani* have a radio?'

'Oh Christ,' I thought, 'it's going to be one of those journeys.'

The darkness of Taoudenni ended for me the following morning, or so I thought. The Commandant and the Adjutant rode up in the Red Cross Land-Rover and took me and my baggage to the transit area, where Hotan's caravan was being loaded up. Omar, Dermas, and the Half-Child were waiting there to see me off.

As Hotan's caravan was being loaded, a collection of soldiers had gathered to wish me well. Beyond them a cluster of miners were looking on with indifferent curiosity. Hotan walked up with his long, loose strides. I said goodbye to my three travelling companions. It was a sad moment. I had learnt much from them, far more than I could have learnt from any book.

Then Hotan gave the Commandant one last para-military salute, took me by the hand, and led me off to the caravan. I saddled my new camel and mounted him. Hotan gave a guttural shout and sixty camels moved off to the south. The heady draughts of desert air blew hard across my face. The sun shone down brilliantly. I felt cleansed and exhilarated. I thought that I had left the darkness behind me.

6

The Caravan of Salt

The sixty camels, in three columns, rambled southwards towards Timbuktu. At the southern end of the salt-pan was a chain of dunes, and hidden away behind those dunes was the concentration camp which I had been forbidden to visit. As we snaked our way through them, I tried to put the darkness of Taoudenni out of my mind. I couldn't. The two Tuareg beasts of burden, the group of camel dung collectors, the dying man, and the grinning adjutant: they haunted me with their degraded faces, as the Sous-Préfet and John Davidson had haunted me on my way to Taoudenni. In Europe they would have been my conscience. Here they were my djinns.

Beyond the chain of dunes the desert was far more like the desert of popular imagination than anything that I had so far encountered. The gentle khaki hills were covered by waves of hardened sand, and rolled away to the south as we moved up and down them. Occasional wedges of jet black rock slashed their way through the free and easy landscape, and above our heads a clear and undulating blue sky stretched from one horizon to the other.

The sixty camels wound through the hills in perfect rhythm, like a well-disciplined crocodile of schoolchildren. The caravan was made up of two separate groups. One, of thirty camels, was led by Hotan and crewed by his son, Lulai, and myself. The other was led by Hedi, a kinsman of Hotan, and crewed by Mohammed, Hedi's brother, and a small black boy, who did not seem to have a name. The two caravans had joined together to provide mutual protection from the almost waterless Tanezrouft Desert and the bandits who were rumoured to be lying in wait for caravans at the *Foum el Alba*, the Pass through the Dunes.

The sixty camels moved in silence, their mouths muzzled to

prevent them licking the salt blocks of the camel in front of them. Each carried four blocks of salt, two on either side of his hump. Each block was five feet long, two feet wide, and one and a half inches thick. Though they had been cut by hand, they were as uniform in their measurements as if they had been machine-made. The blocks, weighing about a hundred and twenty pounds each, were secured by plaited strips of rawhide. Between the salt blocks and the camel's hump was a makeshift pack saddle made of straw, to protect the camel's skin from sores.

The caravans had hardly changed since René Caillié saw them a hundred and fifty years earlier:

The cakes of salt are tied together with cords, made of a sort of grass which grows in the neighbourhood of Tandaye. This grass is dry when gathered; but it is afterwards moistened, and then buried in the ground to keep it from the sun and the east wind, which would dry it too rapidly. When sufficiently impregnated with moisture, it is taken out of the earth and plaited into cords, which the Moors use for various purposes. The camels frequently throw their loads off their backs, and when the cakes of salt arrive in the town they are frequently broken. This would spoil their sale, if the merchants did not take the precaution of joining them together again. When the pieces are fastened together, the cakes are packed up again with a stronger kind of cord made of bull's hide. The cakes are ornamented with little designs, such as stripes, lozenges, etc., traced in black. The slaves are very fond of executing these ornaments, an employment that allows them to collect a little supply of salt for their own use.[1]

As we rumbled on, Hotan called out to me.

'*Nasrani, Nasrani*,' he shouted, pointing due south with confidence. 'Straight ahead for Timbuktu. A little too much to one side, or a little too much to the other side, and you will go to hell.' Then he paused for a moment. 'But with Hotan, *Nasrani*, you will not go to hell. Have confidence in Hotan, *Nasrani*. He is a good guide, and he will take you to Timbuktu in safety.'

But in truth, there was no need for a guide to Timbuktu. The

[1] Caillié, *op. cit.*, Vol. II.

Timbuktu–Taoudenni Road was a well-defined track, as wide as a Clearway, and as straight as a Roman road. How many hundreds of thousands of camels had passed this way, I do not know. The road was covered in camel tracks, camel droppings, and camel bones. All you had to do to get to Timbuktu was to follow the tracks, the bones, and the dung. Twice that day we passed caravans on their way up to Taoudenni, and hardly a day went past without meeting some caravan going north. Coming off the Taghaza Road onto the Timbuktu–Taoudenni Road was like coming off an empty country lane onto a motorway.

I will never forget the first caravan that I saw on the road. It was a magnificent sight, emerging out of the horizon's shimmering heat towards us. The two caravan crews waved and shouted at each other in joy, as Richard Henry Dana recounts sailing ships' crews doing when their ships passed on the open sea. [2] They never slowed from their relentless pace of two and a half miles an hour, but as they neared each other they threw out greetings and gossip, until they passed and finally disappeared, their shapes merging into the nebulous horizon, their voices fading into the roaring trade winds.

The caravan crews, all Berebish tribesmen, knew each other by name. The Berebish have a complete monopoly of the salt traffic between Taoudenni and Timbuktu. They do not actually buy and sell the salt, nor are they paid for the transportation of it with money. Instead they take one fifth of the salt that they carry, and sell it in Timbuktu in lieu of payment.

We did not stop when we met other caravans on the road; we never stopped. From early morning until late at night, we kept on going at the same pace of two and a half miles an hour, until we had come to the end of the Tanezrouft. When the time came for prayers, the crew took it in turns to jump off their camels, bow down to Allah at the side of the track, and run back to the moving caravan, hoisting themselves up onto their moving camels, so that the next man could jump down and do the same.

We did not even stop for midday refreshments. Instead, when the time came for tea, the little black boy without a name would

[2] R. H. Dana, *Two Years Before the Mast*, 1840.

jump off his camel, grab a wooden bowl, and hand it up to Hedi, who would fill it with a mixture of water and millet, to which he added a little salt. This bitter but refreshing drink, which was called *dokhnou*, was passed round to each of us in turn by the black boy, who dodged in and out of the moving columns of camels with the bowl, never spilling a drop.

Most extraordinary of all was the Berebish's improvisation for the tea ceremony. Hotan lit a fire of dried camel dung inside the cooking pot that hung underneath his camel. Then he balanced his blackened kettle on the swinging pot, and when the kettle boiled, he made the tea, sitting on top of his camel. Hotan tasted the tea, pronounced it satisfactory, and then the black boy was called over to hand out the steaming glasses of tea: once, twice, three times. Always three. It was like the Holy Trinity. The first glass tasted good, the second one tasted better, and the third would always be gulped down with a pang of disappointment, knowing there was no more to follow.

Tahar Omar, perhaps out of a sense of guilt for the camel that he had sold me, had personally chosen the second camel that would take me to Timbuktu. From the very beginning of that first journey I had known that there was something wrong with *Mr Wilson*. I could make no such complaint about this second mount. He was no carthorse with a hump, trained to carry a passenger. He was a proper dromedary, twice as tall as my first camel and, from his nervous springy steps, twice as fast. Sitting on that camel, with a cigarette in my mouth and the wind blowing around me, I did indeed feel like a vice-regent, 'turbulent, predatory, elusive and unassailable'. I was all those things.

Of the sixty camels in the caravan, mine was the only one that carried a saddle. My travelling companions had no use for such a cumbersome contraption. Instead they flung blankets over the camels' humps and sat on top, like the Tradjakant. None of them had any difficulty in mounting their moving camels. They simply grabbed the camel's ear as it walked along, pulling the head down and hauling themselves up onto the camel's neck. As the camel raised his neck in protest, they simply slid down onto the hump, twisting themselves into a sitting position as they slid. At first Hotan insisted on giving me a leg up when I wanted to mount.

He meant it as a kindness. But, remembering the Sous-Préfet's advice to 'do as they do', I found this humiliating. So instead I tried to 'do as they do'. The first time I tried it, I ended up flat on my face. After several more similar attempts I managed a successful mount. The nomads cheered and clapped in encouragement.

'You are now a true nomad,' Hedi said. Arabs are great flatterers.

So, mounted, I rode on. It was a memorable day, for I learnt more than just how to mount a moving camel. I learnt about the men that I was travelling with, about their sense of belonging and their harsh vision of life.

Hotan was not only unlike Omar physically, he was also unlike Omar mentally. While Omar was proud, sharp, and quick to batter me into submission, Hotan was grovelling, slow-witted, and totally unsure of himself in the presence of a *nasrani*. Omar had accepted me on his caravan because the Sous-Préfet of Tindouf had told him to, and because I was a useful source of income. Hotan, on the other hand, took me on because I was a status symbol who could enhance his reputation among his fellow nomads. Hardly a caravan went by without Hotan boasting of the important *nasrani* whom he was personally conducting to Timbuktu—a dangerous habit on a route that was rumoured to be visited by bandits. Of course, he never thought of that. He was a simple soul, forever marvelling at my possessions and trying to cadge from me what was not his. As a result, I found him an easy scapegoat to vent my anger and frustrations upon.

Lulai, his plump and obnoxious fourteen-year-old son, had all the worse characteristics of his father, without the saving graces of affection and good-nature. He was a sniffler and a sniggerer, continually spying on me and going through my possessions when he thought that I was not looking. Moreover, he was lazy, greedy, and selfish: three characteristics that I never found in any other Sahara nomad. He was always disappearing when there was work to be done, he ate far more food than anyone else, and he had a nasty habit of stealing other people's sugar.

'Until we reach Timbuktu,' threatened Hotan, 'you will be a son to me, justl ike Lulai. And when we get to Timbuktu, you will meet another son of mine, Nagem.' It was not a prospect that I looked forward to.

Hedi, the master of the second caravan, was a short, sturdy man of middle age, with a beak nose and a goatee beard. He was the strongest and most decisive man on the entire caravan, a natural leader to whom all important decisions were deferred. If nomads in general are an extraordinary combination of opposites, then Hedi was the most extraordinary combination of them all. One moment he was proud, austere, arrogant, and cruel: the next moment he was kind, generous, warm-hearted, and sentimental. Unlike either Hotan or his son, Lulai, Hedi never asked for anything that was not his; yet he would be the first to jump off his camel and search in the sand for the stub of a cigarette that I had carelessly thrown away.

Mohammed, his brother, was a younger man of about my own age. His hair and beard were matted black, and his eyes were deeply set in his dark face. He had the strength of an ox but the mentality of a child, and he was forever singing. With more goodwill than grace, he sang to Allah to keep the camels in good health, to keep us in good health, and—when night dropped down like a safety curtain—to keep the moon in good health, so that we could ride to Timbuktu in safety. It was impossible not to like the man.

As for the black boy without a name, he was just a black boy without a name. Too young to have formed a personality, too old to be patronized as a baby, and too grasping to draw out of me the affection and respect that I had felt for the Half-Child, he was just a black boy, an extra who plays little part in this story. At times I even forgot that he was there.

In the early days at Chegga I had learnt to adapt myself to the ways of the Tradjakant, and to slow down to the rhythm of their lives. I had seen their ways as the most primitive, and their lives as the most basic. Little did I realize that the Tradjakant were extremely sophisticated by nomad standards. With Hotan and Hedi I was taken into an even more primitive world, a world without radios, and a world so far removed from my own that there were times when I feared I would never emerge from it again.

It never occurred to these people that there could be any other world but the one they knew, or that there could be any other way of doing things than the way that they were accustomed. They called the Sahara 'the Sands', as if there were no other sands anywhere in the world. They were visibly shocked when they saw me urinate standing up, and Hotan wondered if I was some sort of spastic because I did not squat as they did, and as Allah told them to. The second time I peed that day, I discovered a very good reason for Allah's instructions. A gust of wind blew right at me, soaking me from the waist downwards.

By the time my clothes were dry, the blue sky had turned grey, the grey had turned dusk red, and the red had turned black. Only then did we swing off the Taoudenni–Timbuktu road into a depression in the hills where, two weeks earlier, Hotan had dumped fodder on his way up to Taoudenni. As we wound our way down into the depression, I could vaguely see in the darkness two stashes of fodder and hundreds of grey balls of dried camel dung all around. It was like a motorway café that no one had bothered to clean up. Hotan told me that the Tanezrouft was so utterly devoid of grazing that the caravans leave fodder at pre-arranged dumps where they stop for the night. By an unspoken agreement among the Berebish, no caravan steals fodder from another's dump.

It was a cold and lonely night. I stared up at the stars, as lifeless as the desert that surrounded me, and shivered in the immensity. Squatting around their fire, the nomads were shouting with accents that I could not understand. Listening to them, I felt distant and alienated. Their voices pierced the air, 'like nothing on earth—it could be bats screeching'.[3]

I watched Hotan cook the meal. It was the same vile menu of rice and camel meat that I had eaten with Omar. How I yearned for a tin of anything. I noticed ominously that there was far less meat in Hotan's pot than there was in Omar's; and what meat there was, was stringy and lined with gristle. As I sat there looking at him cook, Hotan turned to me.

'Cigarette.'

I pretended not to hear.

[3] Herodotus, *The History*, Vol. IV.

'Cigarette.'

Again I took no notice.

'Hey! Hey! *Nasrani*, cigarette. A cigarette for Hotan.'

I gave up, and took out a cigarette from the pack with its brand name 'Liberté'. We passed it round the assembled company like a joint. After it was finished, Hedi put the butt into his pipe and passed that round too. When it was finally dead, Hotan asked for another.

'Cigarette.'

I tried to think what it would be like if Hotan had never existed.

'Hey! *Nasrani*. Another cigarette.'

It was not that I wanted to keep my cigarettes for myself. In Africa it is morally and socially impossible to keep cigarettes for yourself. But I was anxious that the few cigarettes that I had should be spread out over the entire journey.

'If we have another cigarette, Hotan, then there will not be enough cigarettes to get us to Bou Jheba, let alone Timbuktu.' (Bou Jheba was the first village that we would come to after the Tanezrouft.)

'There will be cigarettes in Bou Jheba, *Inshallah*,' said Hotan confidently. 'Many, many cigarettes in Bou Jheba. Too many cigarettes in Bou Jheba.'

I reminded him that it might be God's will that there were no cigarettes in Bou Jheba at all.

Then the old, worn out argument came up.

'But you, *Nasrani*, you have many, many cigarettes. You have too many cigarettes. While I, Hotan, a poor man, I have no cigarettes.'

'If I have too many cigarettes, Hotan, then it must be God's will that I should have too many cigarettes. If I were to give you cigarettes, Hotan, then I would be going against God's will, and you cannot expect me to do that.'

Hotan was dumbfounded by my argument. He did not know what to say. Hedi laughed. I think that he was amused by my blasphemy.

I woke up next morning amid lines of couched camels. In front of the camels the sand had been dug up by their knees, and behind them were mounds of fresh camel droppings, black and shining as olives. It took two hours to load the camels. We worked in groups of two, picking up the blocks of salt, two at a time, and heaving them onto the camels' humps. It was hard work. These nomads work for their one-fifth.

We moved over the same hilly landscape as on the day before, and went through the same routine with prayers, *dokhnou* and tea, until we reached our grazing spot for the night. There is nothing else to say about that day. It was so mundane that I cannot think of even one abnormal incident that would make it interesting. I was so bored I started reading my passport.

'Tomorrow, *Inshallah*,' said Hotan while we were unloading, 'we will reach the well of Bir Ounane. After that there will be no water until we reach the Soudan.' That remark was about the most interesting event of the day.

The next day we travelled over land that was slightly flatter than before. It was a depressing day. After Bir Ounane, there would be a waterless stretch of fifteen days, and I was in no state for such a journey. The chronic diarrhoea that I had contracted at Taoudenni had not gone away. I felt weak and demoralized. The sickness in my body was spreading to my mind. I hoped that the fresh, unbrackish waters of Bir Ounane might cure my dysentery but I was not optimistic. I had lost both my appetite and my sense of enthusiasm. Besides, I was weary of being a stranger among these primitive people. My medicines, which had proved useless against the vile waters of Taoudenni, had become, in my mind, a sick joke. I was swaying around in my saddle, weak from the vacuum in my bowels. I tried not to think of that 'desert within a desert', as Monod called it, that lay ahead.

As the day mellowed I saw ahead of me a high mountain.

'*Ghelb el Ahib*,' said Hotan, betraying all the worse vices of a tourist guide. 'Heart of the Slave.'

I rode on in a depressed silence. No, I had not left the darkness of Taoudenni behind me.

A little beyond the 'Heart of the Slave' we entered a rocky chasm. Here, hidden in these rocks, was the water-hole of Bir Ounane. In the half-light of early night I could see the ruins of fortifications that had been put up by the caravans for protection

from bandits. I unrolled my sleeping-bag and lay down to sleep.
I didn't want to eat. I didn't want to talk. All I wanted was to be
somewhere else.

I woke up next morning and, climbing up onto the fortifications
of Bir Ouane, I turned towards the south. It was an ominous
sight. All I could see was an endless level plain, strewn with
gravel and utterly desolate. There was no undulation nor any
trace of erosion. It was implacably uniform, with the circle of
the horizon as regular as that of an ocean. There was not a stain
to be seen. This was the Tanezrouft proper, the oldest part of the
Sahara Desert, and because it was the oldest, it was also the driest.
I dreaded the journey ahead.

Hotan, who had seen me climbing up onto the rocks and the
parapets, came up and joined me.

'How far does THAT go?' I said.

'Forever,' he replied. Then he decided to be more explicit.
'Until Bou Jheba, *Inshallah*.'

'Fifteen days?'

'Fifteen days, *Inshallah*.'

René Caillié had crossed the Tanezrouft on almost the same
route, going from south to north:

> Our caravan was numerous: it consisted of fourteen hundred
> camels, laden with the various productions of the Soudan; as
> gold, slaves, ivory, gum, ostrich-feathers, and cloth in the
> piece and made into dresses. . . . On leaving Mourat, the
> traveller comes to some deep wells filled with brackish water.
> Here our caravan stopped and took a hearty draught, for we
> were now about to enter upon a part of the desert where we
> should find no water for the space of eight days. In the midst
> of these vast deserts, the wells of Mourat, surrounded by
> fourteen hundred camels, and by the four hundred men of our
> caravan, who were crowded around them, presented the
> moving picture of a populous town; it was a perfect tumult of
> men and beasts. On one side were camels laden with ivory,
> gum, and bales of goods of all sorts; on the other, camels
> carrying on their backs negroes, men, women, and children,

who were on their way to be sold at the Morocco market; and further on, men prostrate on the ground, invoking the prophet.

This spectacle touched and excited my feelings, and in imitation of the devout Musalmans, I fell on my knees; but it was to pray to the God of the Christians: with my eyes turned to the north, towards my country, my relations, and friends, I besought the Almighty to remove from my path the obstacles which had stopped so many other travellers; in the ardour of my wishes, I imagined that my prayers were granted, and that I should be the first European who had set out from the south of Africa [sic] to cross this ocean of sand, and succeeded in the undertaking. The thought electrified me; and while the gloom hung on all other faces, mine was radiant with hope and joy. Full of these sentiments I hastened to mount my camel, and to penetrate fearlessly into the deserts which separate the fertile Soudan from the regions of northern Africa. I felt as if I was mounting the breach of some impregnable fort, and that it was incumbent upon me to sustain the honour of my nation, by diverting myself of every kind of fear and braving this new peril.

A boundless horizon was already expanded before us, and we could distinguish nothing but an immense plain of shining sand, and over it a burning sky. At this sight the camels uttered long moans, the slaves became sullen and silent, and, with their eyes turned towards heaven, they appeared to be tortured with regret for the loss of their country, and with the recollection of the verdant plains from which avarice and cruelty had snatched them. [4]

It took all morning to water the camels and prepare them for the long march across the Tanezrouft. Since our grazing was waiting for us at pre-arranged dumps, there was no way in which we could catch up on those lost hours we spent watering. And so began a series of late starts and long night rides that continued all the way to the Foum el Alba.

We left at midday. The heat of the sun fell down on us, its burning rays destroying all sound, all motion, all rational thought.

[4] Caillié, op. cit., Vol. II.

The stillness and the silence were overwhelming. Strength and resolution were powerless against it. I felt totally defeated, going off on long mind-voyages with a feeling of being lost among shapeless things. Even flight was useless.

The plain that we were travelling across was so flat and feature-less that its horizon played tricks on your eyes. Sometimes it seemed to be an infinity away; at other times it was so close that you could almost touch it. It was completely devoid of all land-marks, disorientating the mind and robbing you of what sense of time and space you still had. It was so bleak and flat that there was no sense of movement. Though we rode for hours, we might just as well have stood still, for all the changes there were in the landscape.

No one talked through those still and brilliant hours of noon and afternoon. Mohammed did not even sing. Each person rode or walked completely alone. It was not until late afternoon, when the sun slid down the sky, that our senses were awakened and we re-discovered each other again.

We rode well into the night. It was freezing cold, and the vindictive north-east wind cut deep into my bones. I sat hunched in my saddle shivering, praying that soon we would reach our prearranged camp. When we finally stopped, the Morning Star was already in the sky, and by the time we had eaten, drunk tea, and passed around a single reassuring cigarette, the sky was turning a battleship grey and another day had begun.

It was a 'heavy' day. So 'heavy' that I had nearly collapsed under its weight. Only Mohammed was able to provide any light relief. As we walked across the undulating emptiness, we tried to make sense to each other with simple words and sign-language.

He was obsessed by motor-cars so, sitting on our camels, we contemplated the miracle of the internal combustion engine.

'Thrum-thrum . . . Motor-cars . . . Too much, too much . . . Motor-cars very beautiful, yes? Very fast, yes? Thrum-thrum.'

He begged me to give him epic accounts of motor-car journeys that I had made. So I told him of one such journey that had begun at South Kensington, taken me westwards down the Cromwell Road, across Hammersmith Fly-over, and onto the M4. I gave the story a touch of colour by adding a description of the Brentford

Nylon factory and an anecdote about a London Airport bus. He stared at me with disbelief. Since he had never seen a bridge, let alone a fly-over, he was clearly impressed by my prowess and daring.

Later I asked Mohammed if he would exchange his camel for a motor-car. He thought about it for a while, unsure of his answer, and then he replied:

'A motor-car is fast and it needs no grazing . . . But if it dies, you cannot eat it. Nor does it breed little motor-cars. No, I would not make the exchange.'

Mohammed was the only nomad in the caravan with whom I had any real contact. I felt apart from the others. The gap between us was wide and unbridgeable. I became increasingly intolerant towards my companions. I was beginning to see everything in terms of 'them' and 'me'. In short, I was becoming just another white racialist. And as my judgements became increasingly those of a racialist, so the darkness became increasingly impenetrable.

The days that followed repeated themselves. Our routine was as regular as clockwork. Yet I was grateful for that routine. It gave form and substance to those dull, dateless days, and gave me the only security that I had.

I remember things on different levels.

I would awake each morning to Hotan's call to prayer, its lingering beauty bringing me into consciousness and taking me from my dreams into other dreams. Then, invariably, Hotan spoilt it all with his ridiculous para-military salute.

After prayers the black boy collected up a pile of dried-up camel dung, and we built a fire and made tea. By the time the tea had been drunk and the camels had been loaded, it was mid-morning. The hours spent drinking tea were always pleasant. The cool air kept the mind clear, and as the morning mist faded away, I would feel that there was no journey that could not be accomplished, no desert that could not be crossed.

Then the journey began. By eleven o'clock I could feel the heat closing in, and could hear the sun raining down on my brain in silence. With every step I would be pursued by a tumult of jostling thoughts. The thoughts themselves were not numerous, but they were repetitious. They went on and on, always returning and never resolving themselves. It is not worth recalling them in detail. They were too subjective to have any interest for a sane person. It is enough to say that even for me they were as dull as the desert that we were travelling through.

> O the mind, mind has mountains; cliffs of fall
> Frightful, sheer, no-man-fathomed.[5]

My mind went back to Helen Waddell's *Lives of the Desert Fathers*.

> It is akin to dejection and especially felt by wandering monks and solitaries, a persistent and obnoxious enemy of such as dwell in the desert . . . like a fever mounting at a regular time, and bringing its highest tide of inflammation at definite accustomed hours to the sick soul.[6]

Was this 'the demon of the noon-tide'? What I had feared ever since seeing the Holy Fool stand up to his god on the *hammada* at Tindouf? If it was, then I was not the only one to be suffering from it. The entire caravan was afflicted, 'at definite accustomed hours'.

By five o'clock, when the 'demon of the noon-tide' departed, the caravan came to life again. Hedi filled his pipe with a discarded cigarette butt, Hotan tried to cadge a cigarette, Lulai started to bully the black boy, and Mohammed began to sing. Only the *nasrani* remained silent, drowned in a depression deeper than anything he had ever encountered. And so it would go on until the early hours of the morning, when we would swing off the road to our fodder dump for that night, and I thanked Allah that another day was over.

Around the camp fire the nomads squawked like Herodotus' bats. Usually I remained silent. When I did speak, the words that came out seemed lifeless, trivial, and indifferent things.

'What are the price of camels in England?' Hotan once asked me.

'There are no camels in England.'

[5] Gerard Manley Hopkins, *Poems (1876–1889)*.
[6] Waddell, *op. cit.*

'But there are motor-cars,' butted in Mohammed. 'There are more motor-cars in England than there are camels in "the Sands". Is that not right, *Nasrani*?'

'Where is England?' Hotan once asked.

'Is it next to Morocco?' put in Hedi.

'No, it is further than Morocco.'

'How much further?'

I made a brief calculation. We were due south of Barnstable. (God, what a thought.)

'If you follow *Bel Hardi*,' I said, 'then you will eventually end up in England.'

It was all getting very complicated, and my schoolboy Arabic was unable to cope. Apparently, somewhere along my answer, there was a misunderstanding. Hotan thought I said that England was even further away than *Bel Hardi*. I tried to put him right, but I only made it worse. So I gave up. Quite clearly the world is divided up into those with radios, and those without them.

I passed round a cigarette. Hotan asked for another. I told him that it was God's will that he should have no more cigarettes. Hotan sulked off like a kicked dog.

Petty as these exchanges seem now, they assumed great importance at the time. My temper was on edge, and I was suffering from acute paranoia, one of the most common diseases suffered by Europeans in Africa.

The fault was mine, I admit. There was much good in these nomads. Men without radios may know less about the world, but they are also freer of the world. To radioless nomads, strangers are still strange, and what lies beyond their immediate experience is still a marvel and a mystery. They may cadge and they may beg, but they do it without shame and without hypocrisy.

The days crawled on and the miles creaked by, the sixty camels silently shuffling southwards across an empty world. Inside that emptiness I felt imprisoned, my eyes fixed towards Timbuktu, as a prisoner's eyes are fixed rigidly on the door of his cell.

Until the sixth day out of Taoudenni. That night we did not stop. We rode on through the night, under a moon that gave the desert a silver hue. I asked Hotan why we had not stopped. 'Bandits,' he said. The bandits, he explained, came from El Juf, the Belly, an empty quarter of Mauritania close to the frontier with Mali. They lay in wait for the caravans at the Foum el Alba, and then escaped across the border into Mauritania.

It was easy to disbelieve. It was easy to disbelieve most of the things that Hotan told me. But my total lack of respect for Hotan's truthfulness did not reassure me. Omar, too, had told me of bandits in this part of the Sahara, and it was the best spot that bandits could choose to attack caravans. The Foum el Alba was a great pass through a range of sand dunes that ran from east to west, right across the Tanezrouft. It was the only way through this 'desert within a desert'. No camel, no caravan, not even a Land-Rover, could move across the Tanezrouft without going through the pass. I wound my turban (or *howli*, as it is called in the vernacular) around my face to look like an Arab.

We rode on and on through the night, under a moon that moved across the darkness above us as we rode. About two hours after Hotan had told me about the bandits, he asked me if I carried a gun. Considering his obnoxious son had been through my luggage several times, I almost told him to ask Lulai.

'No, Hotan, I do not have a gun.'

'A great pity,' he said, and rode on in a disappointed silence.

Suddenly we came to a great wall of sand, hundreds of feet high. Hotan swung the caravan to the west. For two miles we rode parallel to the sand wall until we came to an opening. The pass was almost a mile across, narrowing to less than a quarter of a mile at the centre. This was the Foum el Alba, the great bottleneck of the Tanezrouft. We rode through the pass in total silence, the only sound being the creaking of the salt blocks rubbing against each other as the camels moved, the only sight being the rectangular blocks of salt, luminous and glowing in the night.

I yearned for Algeria, where justice reigned and roads were not lawless.

By the time we came out of the pass, the melodrama had worn thin. The bandits had failed to materialize. (Since Hotan had introduced the subject to me, I should have expected them to fail to materialize.) Dawn was coming up, and on the ground I could see the tracks of camels and gazelle. It made sense. If man was forced to use this pass, then animals were forced to use it also. I was surprised, however, that in a desert as bleak as this, animals like gazelle should be able to exist.

I questioned Hedi about the tracks.

'Yes, many animals use this pass. Too many,' and he laughed.

'No bandits?' I asked. (He had not even mentioned bandits.)

'Oh yes, there are bandits. But they are not interested in us. We are carrying salt, and there is too much salt in "the Sands". What they want are the caravans of tea and sugar that go UP to Taoudenni, not the salt that comes DOWN.'

I started laughing, not because I was amused, but to release the tension that had been building up in me. All that bullshit from Hotan about bandits attacking us, all those questions about whether I was carrying a gun. He knew perfectly well that we were completely safe. What he was interested in were those wild animal tracks. He hoped that we might be able to do a little eco-logical banditry of our own, and have fresh meat for tomorrow.

We rode on for another hour. It was a steel grey morning, bitter cold. We were riding, so Hedi told me, to some grazing, the only grazing in the Tanezrouft. The sun was high up in the sky by the time we reached it. It was nothing more than a few mean and ugly shoots of khaki green shrub, yet it held promise and hope, and for a mere twenty-four hours, it kept back the terrible depression threatening to drown me.

We stayed on that patch of grazing all the next day. Hotan and Mohammed, who had been scratching themselves throughout the entire journey, were now delicately picking out lice from the folds of their clothing, then squeezing them to death between bloody fingernails. After killing his lice, Hotan began sewing up the rents in his clothing, using his toes as extra fingers, like a well-trained spastic. How I hated that man.

We left the next morning over the same flat, monotonous landscape, as bleak and boring as a concrete wall. Even the mirages repeated themselves. The north-eastern wind flushed across the empty *reg*, bringing lines of dancing djinns in its wake.

We had swung off the main Taoudenni–Timbuktu road that

continued due south to Arouan and Timbuktu, and were moving
in a south-south-easterly direction towards Bou Jheba and Guir,
where Hedi's encampment was. Right up until this point, not a
day had gone by without us meeting a caravan going towards
Taoudenni. From now until we reached the steppes of the
Soudan, we did not see another living soul.

The days that followed were a lonely nightmare. I was rapidly
losing confidence in my own horizons.

I found I was going deeper into my 'inner journey', a journey
into my own past, catching a landmark here, an obstacle there.
As I rode on through the terrible Tanezrouft, the djinns of my
past were as real as the djinns of sand that slashed at my legs and
stung my eyes. The further I went in that undulating emptiness,
the deeper I went on a journey into the past, reliving the successes
and failures, the achievements and false starts, the acts of betrayal
and the acts of love that had made me what I was.

Santayana has said that an Englishman is governed by the
weather of his soul. If that is so, then my weather ranged from
calms of total apathy to raging storms of mental agonies. I
walked and rode across the empty plain with a mind that was
either drowned in total indifference, or upside-down in senseless
upheavals. Where would such weather lead me? To the Sous-
Préfet's shadow of a shadow of a smile, or to the Holy Fool's
madness? I found no answer; I could only hope, as the lights of
my universe went out, one by one.

'Oh my God, oh my God. Why hast Thou forsaken me?'

More and more I found myself seeking refuge in my own
journal. Reading it over now, it makes little sense. Hopelessness
and self-hatred dominate the pages. The main impression is one of
incoherence—half-hearted attempts to find order in the heap of
dried-up images around me—and meaningless attempts to justify
myself. Yet those hours I spent writing were not entirely useless.
They saved me from that dangerous game of talking to myself,
and kept safe what sanity I still had inside me.

The days repeated themselves endlessly. The occasional incident
that punctuated the days was the only thing that made it possible
to distinguish one from another.

Three incidents, particularly, dominate my memory. The first of these was the strangest of all. Walking across the empty plain, I saw ahead of me a line of hoof-marks. They were travelling in a north-easterly direction. I did not imagine them, because Hedi saw them also. He even pointed them out to me. Where were they going to? Where were they coming from? I just do not know. I asked Hedi, but he only shrugged his shoulders, and said they were probably going to Hell. I got no more out of him. The mystery remains unsolved.

The second and third incidents both happened at night. The second happened around the camp-fire. Lulai had captured a desert mouse, and was holding it above the fire by its tail, gently singeing it. The entire encampment was roaring with laughter at this callous brutality. Watching the pathetic animal struggle, I could take it no more. I screamed at Lulai to stop, telling him, in my inadequate pidgin Arabic, that whatever he did to that mouse, I would do to him.

There was silence. The camp was as still as a photograph. I saw the nomads studying me quietly, their eyes watchful and cruel. For a moment I was frightened.

Slowly Lulai put the animal down. It scampered away into the darkness.

The silence remained, until Hotan broke it.

'That was the right thing to do,' he said. 'You are a good *nasrani*.'

I think that I despised him for that more than for anything else.

The last of the incidents happened while we were riding through the night. It was bitter cold, so I took my jeans out of my saddle bag and tried to put them on, still sitting on my camel.

'You can't do that,' said Hotan. 'The camels aren't used to trousers. Trousers will scare them.'

It sounds funny now, but it provided no light relief at the time. It just reinforced my own sense of cultural alienation. Boredom and apathy dominated the days, and loneliness and sleeplessness dominated the nights.

My physical state reflected my mental state. My lips were cracked and lacerated, my body was covered in sores, and dysentery had reduced it to a skeleton. I had completely lost my appetite.

Mounting my camel one morning, I heard a banging sound like a muffled hammer hitting wood. I felt a sharp jab of pain at the bottom of my spine and felt my thighs with my fingers. The folds of flesh had all but disappeared; there was nothing but bones covered by an apology of bruised skin.

Later that day I fainted. I don't remember much about it. One moment I was swaying around in my saddle, the next I was on the ground, looking up at Hotan holding a bowl of water. He lowered the bowl to my lips and slowly raised it up, letting the water gurgle into my mouth. Then he lifted me gently up onto my camel. As we rode along, I noticed that Mohammed had added another verse to his song. He was singing to Allah to keep the *nasrani* strong, so that he would get to Timbuktu in safety. I overtook him in silence; inwardly I was crying.

I am not sure exactly of the chronology of the events that followed. My journal is of little help. But two events happened that marked a great change in me.

The first happened sometime between my fainting and my arrival at the steppes of the Soudan. I was squatting by the campfire, shivering with cold. The nomads had either blankets or bernouses (nomad capes) to protect them from the cold, but I had nothing but an inadequate jersey. My teeth were chattering and my body was numb. Seeing me shivering, Hotan offered me a share of his blanket.

'While you are with me, *Nasrani*, you are like a son. The same as Lulai.'

I squirmed at the idea, but I could not refuse. Hotan's blanket crawled with lice and was caked in snot, but there are things more important than someone else's lice and mucus. The bond of human solidarity had been stretched out to me, and I could not refuse. Within a few minutes Hotan's blanket had warmed my body, as his kindness had warmed my soul.

The second happened the following night. I had drunk some *dokhnou*, and had slid off my camel to relieve my bowels. It was a dark and cloudy night. There was no moon, and *Bel Hardi*, the North Star, was hidden behind a thick blanket of clouds.

Squatting there in the dark, with my *jelaba* (Arab tunic) drawn around me like a tent, I felt dizzy and lost my sense of direction. By the time I had finished, the caravan had disappeared in the darkness. I searched for camel tracks, but I could find none. I called out into the night, but no one responded. I felt alone and frightened. Night was as dark as a bottomless pit. I tried to dig a trench with my fingers, for protection from the night, but it was a hopeless task. There was nothing I could do until morning, when I could follow the caravan's tracks. I reconciled myself to the idea of possible death by exposure and, for a brief moment, I believed that the last light in my universe was about to go out.

Then, suddenly, I heard a cry from out of the darkness.

'Nasrani! Nasrani!'

I shouted back.

'Hamdullah! Hamdullah!'

It was the turn of the other voice now.

'Nasrani! Nasrani!'

'Hamdullah! Hamdullah!'

'Nasrani! Nasrani!'

The voice was getting closer now. We were groping with our voices in the dark. Then I saw a figure on a camel; he was coming out of the dark towards me.

It was Mohammed, coming out of the night, a star shining in the darkness.

He had been riding in the rearguard of the caravan and had noticed me drop out, he told me later. When I had not reappeared, he became worried. So he broke all the rules of the desert by coming back to look for me, risking his own life to save mine.

'Hamdullah!' I repeated. Thanks be to God.

He lowered his arm and braced it. I took it, and he hauled me up behind him on his camel. After a few minutes' gallop, we had reached the caravan again.

I did not place much importance on either incident at the time. No doubt if I had known more about psychiatry, I would have found meaning in them and would have seen them as vital signposts on the road to my mental recovery. But to me, at the time, they were just incidents. I knew no more about the laws of the mind than I knew about the laws of storms.

We reached Guir on the night of 21 December. It was the first water we had come to since Bir Ounane. We were on the same flat plain of gravel that we had been travelling on since Bir Ounane, but there was a difference. We were nearing the end of the Tanezrouft, and a feeling of optimism and expectancy had spread over the entire caravan.

Here Hedi, Mohammed, and the black child were to split off from us with thirty of the camels. They were going to Hedi's encampment close by. Hotan, Lulai, and myself were going on to Hotan's encampment at Tin Tehoun, and from there to Timbuktu. It was a sad moment. I had grown fond of Hedi and Mohammed, particularly Mohammed, with his cheerful mundane courage.

I remember sitting round the camp-fire, exchanging good wishes and hopes of meeting sometime in the future—*Inshallah*. Hotan's and Mohammed's lice had spread throughout the caravan. As we passed around the last of the cigarettes, Hotan began to scratch, then Mohammed scratched, then Hedi . . . and finally, I began to scratch.

We parted company the next afternoon. We loaded up the two caravans, then led our camels in different directions. Hedi and Mohammed gave a wave and swung to the west, finally disappearing over the horizon and out of my life.

Hotan, Lulai, and myself led the other caravan to the south, in the direction of the tiny township of Bou Jheba that sat on the edge of the Tanezrouft Desert. There, Hotan had assured me, I would be able to buy 'many, many cigarettes'.

We rode long into the night until finally setting up our camp. As we unloaded the camels, Hotan made a gesture with his hands around him.

'Here is the end of the Tanezrouft,' he said.

The nightmare was over.

That night I dreamt that I was on the road to Timbuktu. But Omar, Dermas, Hotan, and Hedi had no place on that road, they played no part in the dream. The landmarks on the route were episodes from my past, and the people that I met were characters from that past. Through Tindouf, Chegga, Taoudenni, and the Tanezrouft I travelled my entire quarter century of life, passed the night in 'Free Derry' when the tanks smashed through the barricades, passed the night when —— was shot, passed the police raid and the prison cell, the terrors of the Trip that went wrong, and the terrors of my first day at school, and so on, passed all the other wounds and humiliations of childhood. And then I went even further back, until I reached that bright red fire-engine, my earliest recollection. And further still, until I had reached the very beginning, the primal point. Only then, after I had encountered and confronted every djinn of my past, did I realize that there was nothing more to be frightened of. There was nowhere further to go back, nowhere to go but forward.

'And God said, "Let there be light": and there was light.'[7]

We were camped on the very edge of the Tanezrouft. Behind us was the bleak and sterile plain of gravel that we had been travelling on for so long. In front were the steppes of the Soudan.

I could see a long line of trees stretched across the horizon. Behind the trees was verdant grassland. There were birds in the trees, birds in the sky, birds pecking and strutting on the ground. I could see cows grazing among the trees. The mosque of Bou Jheba dominated a hill to the west. There seemed to be an awful lot of goats.

I took out my journal and wrote in the date. It was Christmas Eve. I picked up the Koran and flicked through the pages until I reached *Maryam*, and laboriously copied down the text:

So she conceived him, and withdrew with him to a remote place. When the time came the pains of childbirth drove her to the trunk of a palm-tree. Realizing her condition, she cried out: Would that I had died before this and had been quite forgotten. The voice of the angel reached her from below: Grieve not; for thy Lord has provided a rivulet below thee, wherein thou mayst wash thyself and the child. Then take hold of the branch

[7] *Genesis*, I, v. 3.

of the palm-tree and shake it; it will shed fresh ripe dates upon thee. Thus eat and drink and wash and be at rest. Shouldst thou see anyone approaching, call out: I have this day vowed a fast to the Gracious one. I will, therefore, hold no converse with any person.

She accompanied him to her people, while he was riding. They upbraided her: Mary, thou hadst perpetrated an abominable thing. O sister of Aaron, thy father was not a wicked man, nor was thy mother an unchaste woman. She pointed to him. They said: How can we hold converse with one who was but yesterday a child being rocked in a cradle?

Jesus taught: I am a servant of Allah, He has given me the Book, and has appointed me a Prophet; he has made me blessed wheresoever I may be, and has enjoined upon me Prayer and almsgiving throughout my life. He has made me dutiful towards my mother, and has not made me haughty and graceless. Peace was ordained for me the day I was born, the day I shall die and the day I shall be raised up to life again.[8]

The road to Timbuktu will be easier now.

[8] *The Koran*, 19:23–34, trans. M. Z. Khan.

7

The Steppes of the Soudan

We rode into Bou Jheba that Christmas Eve. I remember Bou Jheba as a scrap of a village with no particular streets. Naked children ran out of the houses chanting 'Nasrani! Nasrani!' Women ran away at the sight of me, and goats stared with amazement. I felt supremely happy. I had left the darkness and the desert behind me, and had reached the shores of humanity.

The Marabout of Bou Jheba came out of his house to greet us. He was an old man with a long white beard and a sad, simple face, a Victorian King Lear. He led us into his house and offered us tea and couscous. After we had eaten, he went over to his trunk in the corner of the room and took out an old nineteenth-century portfolio. He unwrapped it with the same treasured care that the Adjutant at Taoudenni had unwrapped his collection of pornographic photographs. The papers inside it were all affidavits from travellers who had passed through Bou Jheba. Some of them were a hundred years old.

There must have been a century of Malian history in that old leather portfolio, and that history had not always been so dark. The oldest pieces of paper were parched and withered. They were written in Arabic and meaningless to me. Next were brief notices written in French by obscure army officers and administrators, stating in cryptic officialese that hospitality had been given and had been gratefully received, and that the taxes of the village had always been paid on time. After them came a collection of African nationalist leaflets, full of slogans and meaningless platitudes about liberty and progress. The date of Malian independence was noted down, so was the arrest of several villagers accused of stealing a donkey, I think. After that there were several letters written in Russian; again, they were meaningless. The last entries were from American oilmen, the most recent imperialists of them all. I put the portfolio down and pitied Africa.

The Marabout of Bou Jheba motioned me to write something down for his collection. What I wrote was simple and to the point. 'On 24 December I was received at Bou Jheba with outstanding hospitality, for which I am very grateful.'

Outside the hut the entire village had gathered. They were fascinated by me. I could see the smiles on the faces of the children in the front, who had ringside seats. Everything that I did was an act. They were talking amongst themselves.

'See the *nasrani* blow his nose on a piece of cloth . . . See the *nasrani* write with a pen . . . See the *nasrani* scratch himself.'

It was theatre to them.

After a while the Marabout became embarrassed by his villagers. The play was over, he seemed to say, and tried to shoo them away. But he wasn't a very awesome marabout. The crowd just laughed and stayed there. He shouted to them to go; they were making an exhibition of themselves in front of a *nasrani*, he said. But the crowd just laughed. They were quite happy making an exhibition of themselves. The Marabout was getting flustered. He did not like to have his authority so outwardly flouted in front of a stranger. He was frightened that the government might hear of it. The crowd was giggling and cackling; the poor man was close to tears.

Finally the village constable appeared. He was a comic constable, a Dogberry. Roaring out oaths, threatening the vengeance of Allah and the force of the law, he drove the crowds away with a big stick. He stood by the door on guard, but even he was a figure of fun. The children taunted him from a distance, chanting his name and throwing stones.

Decorum established, the old Marabout was happy. He invited me to stay to drink tea, and sent off his grandson to fetch the village elders. The little boy, about five years old and with the top of his head shaven like a Red Indian, raced off at the double. He was frightened of losing his privileged seat.

The elders trooped in, one at a time, each one officially waved in by the comic constable. We sat drinking tea in silence. They stared at me as if I was a visitor from outer space. One of them picked his nose, another fingered his worry beads. After the second glass, one of them broke the silence and asked me a question.

'Does the *nasrani* have a radio?'

'No.'

'A great pity.'

'God's will.'

'God's will.'

'Does the *nasrani* have a cigarette?'

'No.'

'A great pity.'

'God's will.'

'God's will.'

The old Marabout called in his grandson. The boy had been outside, giving his friends a minute by minute report on the *nasrani*. The comic constable left his post at the door and ran to a group of giggling boys. He grabbed the grandson by the ear and led him into the hut. The Marabout gave the boy some money and sent him off. The elders of Bou Jheba were nodding in approval.

The boy came back a few minutes later with a battered silver stem pipe and a pouch of tobacco.

'It is for you,' the Marabout said.

I thanked him, and gave him a pocket torch in return. That was the nearest that I got to exchanging Christmas presents.

It was now midday. Hotan arrived to collect me. He had cadged a leg of mutton for the Moslem feast of the killing of the sheep.

I asked Hotan when the feast was.

'Tomorrow,' he said.

Christmas dinner, I thought. I was not too old to disbelieve in miracles.

The next day we ate our Christmas dinner. Moslem and Christian tore into the meat with relish, each celebrating his respective feast. I hadn't eaten a proper meal for two weeks. No Christmas dinner of turkey, sprouts, peas and potatoes, washed down by brandy and champagne, could have tasted quite so good.

We left on Boxing Day, late in the afternoon. The contrast between the Sahara and the Soudan was sudden and spectacular.

The dull and silent landscape of sand and gravel was behind us. We were riding through bushes and trees, past a herd of cows, over a column of ants, and underneath a squadron of squawking birds. A herdsman waved at us, a camel-rider shouted out salutations, and a group of children laughed. On the ground were cows' pats, donkey droppings, even horses' turds. The camel was no longer king.

Then, just as I was thinking that we had arrived in Black Africa, the steppelands fell behind us and we found ourselves back in the desert, labouring up and down rolling hills of soft sand. We trekked through them. Then, just as we were reconciling ourselves to being back in the desert, the steppes reappeared. The desert and the steppes went on playing tricks like that almost all the way to Timbuktu.

By the time darkness fell, we were travelling through a patch of woodland. We stopped by a decayed tree-trunk. We had no more millet, we were low on sugar, and we had only one match left (Hotan having lost his flint in the Tanezrouft). Bou Jheba had been able to supply us with rice, mutton, and tobacco, but they had no matches and no sugar. We were rapidly running out of things to run out of.

'We will stop here,' said Hotan, pointing to the tree-trunk. 'With one match we can keep a fire going until morning.'

We unloaded the thirty camels and prepared a meal of the last of the mutton. Since leaving the Tanezrouft my bowels had stabilized themselves, and I had regained my appetite. We gobbled down the mutton and rice, crushing the bones to suck out the marrow. The grease ran down the sides of our mouths shamelessly.

I fell asleep early, but woke up in the middle of the night. It was warm and windless. I felt neither frightened nor tormented. I had reconciled myself to Hotan, with his strange primitive ways, just as I had reconciled myself to the djinns that had followed me across the Tanezrouft. I looked out at the shadows of landscape around me. It was all very familiar. The ant holes, the thorn bushes, the animal droppings, the lizard tracks, the cracked and parched earth . . . I felt that I had seen it all before, like coming into a town in which, although you have never been there, you seem to know by instinct where the railway station and the pub are.

I had come back to an old memory. I had been here before. I had returned to Africa. It all came back now: the sights, the sounds, the smells, and the feelings. I lay awake in my sleeping-bag, listening to the jackals howl out in the darkness, and as I lay there I let Africa seep back into my consciousness.

That night I dreamt of Africa. It started as a dream about my childhood in Africa, then the dream widened out, becoming a dream about Africa in general. Omar and Hotan appeared briefly in the dream, Omar as a bullying teacher, and Hotan as some simple-minded saint.

When I awoke, I was conscious of a profound change inside me. It came out most noticeably in the total disappearance of tension, and in my new attitude to Hotan. The process that had begun on Christmas Eve was now complete.

That was my first dream about Africa. It marked the complete breakdown of my European defences. I had finally become integrated in my surroundings.

The days that followed were happy, carefree days. I felt a great sense of relief at having left the Tanezrouft behind me. I was now on the home stretch. I had gone far and I had gone deep, further and deeper than I could possibly have imagined. I walked and rode through the steppes of the Soudan, basking in the carelessness, the protectiveness, and the childishness of Africa.

Reading Ibn Battuta's account of his travels in the Soudan, it is impossible not to be impressed by the extent of commercial activity and the stability of the political institutions.

> A traveller in this country carries no provisions whether plain food or seasoning, and neither gold nor seasoning. He takes nothing but pieces of salt and glass ornaments, which the people call beads, and some aromatic goods. [L]

The use of salt as a medium of exchange is not unique to the people of the Soudan. Marco Polo reported in his *Travels* that in several parts of Asia salt was used as currency.

[L] Battuta, *op. cit.*

At Kumbi, Ibn Battuta was granted an audience with the king during a visit by some cannibals from Wangara, the place where the gold was supposed to come from.

The sultan received them without honour, and gave them as his hospitality-gift a servant, a negress. They killed and ate her, and having smeared their faces and hands with her blood came to the sultan to thank him. I was informed that this was their regular custom whenever they visit his court. Someone told me about them that they say that the choicest parts of women's flesh are the palms of the hands and the breasts.'[2]

At Walata, a little to the west of where we were travelling, Ibn Battuta was impressed by the attractiveness of the ladies.

Their women are of surpassing beauty, and are shown more respect than the men. The state of affairs amongst these people is indeed extraordinary. Their men show no sign of jealousy whatever; no one claims descent from their father, but on the contrary from their mother's brother. . . . The women have their own 'friends' and 'companions' amongst the men outside their own families. . . . At Walata I went to the qadi's house, after asking his permission to enter, and found him with a young woman of remarkable beauty. When I saw her I was shocked and turned to go out, but she laughed at me, instead of being overcome by shame.[3]

'One minute in the life of the world is going by,' Cézanne is reported to have said. 'Paint it as it is.' I remember that minute vividly.

Hotan was sitting on his camel, astride the hump, quietly intoning verses of the Koran as he alternated between scratching his lice bites and picking his nose. Lulai was riding at the back of the caravan, silently scratching, and whittling a stick with his father's knife. The *nasrani*, at the front with Hotan, was also silently scratching.

To their left the wind whistled through some bushes; ahead a flock of birds flew away in fright at the caravan's approach.

[2] *Ibid.*   [3] *Ibid.*

Once, during that minute, the *nasrani* stretched his neck and looked behind him. The long line of thirty camels jogged along in pairs; resigned and expressionless, they told you nothing.

The birds had gone now and, apart from the noise of grass-hoppers, there was total silence.

Occasionally on our journey a load shifted and the blocks of salt crashed to the ground. Then Lulai would dismount and run up, and I would dismount and run back, and we would reload the camel as it walked along. Sometimes a lead rope would untie, and a segment of the caravan would be left behind while Lulai at the back shouted to Hotan to stop.

Nothing like that happened during that particular minute. It was all very peaceful.

During those days Hotan was at his best. He cadged, he saved, he made-do. Evidently running out of essential supplies like sugar was no new experience for him.

On our second day out of Bou Jheba, we had only one chunk of sugar left. Hotan carefully broke it into two pieces. One piece we had with our morning tea, the other piece was put away in the saddle-bag.

We passed through the same changing landscape as before, sometimes desert and sometimes steppes. I remember an injured bird running off the track in front of us, its wings flapping help-lessly in panic. I remember a cow, too. And the bones of a gazelle, picked clean by jackals and carrion.

About midday, after prayers, Hotan, searching in his saddle-bag, discovered that the piece of sugar was missing. He looked back at Lulai, who was at the rear of the caravan, accusingly. He waited for about an hour, silent with anger. Then he called Lulai to the front of the caravan. Waiting until Lulai was within range, Hotan picked up his riding whip and struck out at his son. Once, twice, three times. Lulai was writhing on the ground, screaming. His crime had been unforgivable, Hotan later told me.

For two hours Hotan did not speak. Then, seeing some fresh camel tracks ahead of him, he let out a yell of delight.

'Those camel tracks were made this morning,' he said con-fidently. 'There are six camels and five donkeys. One of the camels is lame, and two of the donkeys are very young. All but the two young donkeys are carrying heavy weights. There are two men as well. God willing, they may have sugar and matches to give us.'

He tried to urge the camels on faster, but in vain. It was several hours before the caravan came into sight, and it was not until the time for prayers that we were within hailing distance of them. They stopped and waited for us to catch up.

Sure enough, there were six camels and five donkeys. One of the camels was lame, and two of the donkeys were foals. The caravan was carrying salt to a nearby encampment, part of the continuous local traffic in salt that went on in this part of the Soudan. Each camel carried four blocks of salt, and each donkey carried two blocks. The two youngest donkeys carried nothing at all.

I was impressed by Hotan's skill as a tracker. Compared to him, I was an ecological illiterate.

Hotan was as skilful in his cadging as in his tracking. He had a way with people when he wanted to get something out of them. It had not worked with me, but that was probably because of the language problem and the intense dislike that I felt for Hotan from the start. But it worked with his own people. Years of running out of essentials had moulded him into a first-class sponger.

The first thing that he did when he wanted something, was to make his prospective victim laugh. Then he impressed upon them his own importance. He did this by introducing me as a rich *nasrani* who was travelling with Hotan on important government business. It worked. First the victim laughed, then he stood tongue-tied. That was Hotan's cue.

Had they sugar?

They shook their heads. They had very little sugar.

Hotan tried again.

Would they swop what sugar they had for some tea?

Again they shook their heads. They had too much tea and not enough sugar. In fact, they had been hoping that we could give them some sugar.

But Hotan was not a man to give up easily.

How about tobacco? My tobacco, I should add.

They nodded their heads in agreement.

Hotan promptly handed over half the tobacco that the Marabout at Bou Jheba had given me. In exchange, he got a few measily lumps of sugar. It was hardly a fair deal, but Hotan was overjoyed. We rode off in triumph with our sugar in Hotan's saddle-bag, like tribal warriors returning from battle laden with booty.

That night we got drunk on sweetened tea. Unloading the camels, Lulai had slipped and grazed his elbow. He asked me for *dowa*. I couldn't be bothered to rummage through my baggage looking for medicine, so I rubbed toothpaste on his elbow instead. It worked just as well. An oversized grin spread out on his face and he walked off feeling happy. There was no pain at all, he assured me. He examined his wound for a while, and then he began to lick the peppermint-flavoured toothpaste off his elbow, when he thought that no one was looking.

As we sat round the fire I began to delouse my clothing. It had become a regular nightly occupation. I had almost finished when I heard Lulai scream. I turned around. He was sitting as still as a statue. A scorpion was crawling over the blanket that he had around him. It looked cold and beautiful. It was moving delicately across the folds of wool, and would soon drop down onto his thigh. Silently Hotan picked up his riding whip. With an expert flick he sent the scorpion flying through the air onto the ground. The pale luminous scorpion began to run off into the darkness. But he had no chance. We grabbed blazing embers from the fire and smashed them down on his gem-like body. We burnt him, we broke him, and finally, as he lurched through his last agony, we crushed him.

I slept that night with poison on my mind, and when I was awoken in the small hours of morning by the touch of a desert mouse crawling over my face, I froze with terror.

We left the next day for In Alia. On the road we met three nomads going in the opposite direction. When the first two, sharing one camel between them, came up over the crest of a hill, Hotan let out a scream of delight. I knew what he wanted, for after the customary greeting, he made them laugh, and impressed upon them the importance of the *nasrani* whom he was conducting to Timbuktu.

Then he asked them if they had any sugar to spare.

No. Sugar was hard to come by.

There appeared to be a sugar famine in the Soudan. We rode on in disappointed silence.

About two hours later we met the third nomad, riding a camel towards us. He was a Tuareg, with black curly hair and a blue-tinted veil over his face. A nineteenth-century bayonet and a broadsword hung down from his saddle.

Hotan greeted him with enthusiasm. He told him a joke and introduced him to the *nasrani*.

The Tuareg was silent. Trying again, Hotan made another joke and asked him if he had any sugar.

The Tuareg looked blank.

He could speak no Arabic, only Tamachek, the language of the Tuareg. He stared at us a while, looking even blanker, then rode on without saying a word.

We travelled over gentle rolling hills and scrubby grasslands. Just before dusk, a group of seven gazelles jumped out of a clump of trees in front of us and raced off, with long graceful strides, towards the horizon. It was like riding through Paradise, except that there are no lice in Paradise.

We did not reach the well of In Alia that night. It didn't matter. Nothing really mattered. I lay awake under a full moon, feeling safe and secure in the agelessness of Africa.

We came in sight of In Alia at mid-morning, the next day. It lay on a bleak, windswept hill. As we rode up, an old man and a boy were watering camels and goats. Close by them stood a blind man, staring blankly into the darkness around him. The old man watering the animals looked up at me with friendly curiosity. His skin was as withered as tissue-paper.

'Who is the *nasrani*?' he asked Hotan.

Hotan explained. The old man looked confused.

Then he called over the blind man. He told him there was a *nasrani*.

The blind man greeted me. I replied.

Then he came up to me, following the direction of my voice. He began to feel my legs and hands, seeing me through his fingertips. As he did so, he mumbled something to the old man.

'He wants *dowa*,' the old man said.

'I have no *dowa* that can cure him of his illness,' I said sadly. The blind man listened without comment. Then he took himself off to the shade of a nearby tree. On his face was a pathetic look of disappointment. All that he had wanted was a miracle.

After he had gone, Hotan asked the old man if he had any sugar. He shook his head. He had no sugar, no tea, no tobacco. He had nothing.

Hotan went to his saddle-bag and gave him half the tea. Then he told me to do the same with the tobacco.

We rode on southwards, through steppelands of dried grass and crippled trees.

'Timbuktu very close now,' said Hotan optimistically. 'Timbuktu near, Tanezrouft far. Think that and soon you will be in Timbuktu. Everything you could possibly want is in Timbuktu. Too much of everything.'

I confess I was beginning to like the man, with his uncompromising generosity and uncompromising optimism.

As we rode towards Timbuktu, I tried to build up a mental picture of the place . . . The two mosques, the city rising out of the dunes, the rush of people, and the variety of clothing. All the old clichés were there. And as I built up this picture, I began to understand the mystery of Timbuktu. It may be no more than a scruffy dump where all the luckless debris of African humanity are washed up, a sordid hole with nothing to recommend it but a stamp on a passport and a river boat that ploughs the waters of the Niger and takes you somewhere else, but coming out of the desert, where there is absolutely nothing, Timbuktu offers everything you could possibly want. The Saharan nomads who told an obsessed Europe that on the other side of the desert was a great metropolis that had everything, were not telling lies. Compared to the empty Sahara and the apologies for villages that we had seen in the Soudan, Timbuktu was a great metropolis with everything.

Late that afternoon we came upon another caravan going in the same direction as ourselves. It was small, only six camels carrying salt, and led by a tall, lanky nomad called Yahia. He was a wild-looking, friendly youth, and although he had no sugar, he shared his tobacco with us in an easy-going, generous way. With his black curly hair and deepset eyes, he looked like some minor prophet.

We stopped about a mile from the well of Ouzozil, the last watering place before Hotan's encampment at Tin Tehoun. After we had set up camp, Yahia and Lulai rode off to a nearby encampment to try to cadge sugar. They came back empty-handed, to face a sad, sugarless night. I could not share their disappointment. Without sugar I knew that there would be nothing to stop us reaching Tin Tehoun tomorrow. The relief of escaping from the Tanezrouft had now worn off. I no longer felt supremely happy. I felt good, the next best thing.

Sitting at the camp-fire eating a tealess meal, Hotan told me once again that I was like a son to him. I no longer cringed at the thought; now I took it for what it was, a good-natured compliment.

On 30 December we loaded up the caravan for the last time, and descended down a hill to the well of Ouzozil. A large grey camion was parked by the well. It had been stripped of wheels, tyres, and even cabin. We had reached the suburbs of civilization. I asked Hotan about the camion and what it was doing there. It had broken down years ago, he answered. The nomads now used it to put their livestock in. Nobody had bothered to move it. Nobody cared enough to move it.

At Ouzozil we said goodbye to Yahia; he was going to the well to water his camels. We pressed on. We wanted to be at Tin Tehoun by nightfall.

Hotan, I now realized, was very much a family man. He was continually talking about 'the wife' and 'kids'. He had eight children. They ranged in age from the youngest, three months, to the oldest, Nagem, in his mid-twenties.

After an uneventful day we arrived at the spot where Hotan's encampment had last been. There was nothing there. He looked around him dumbfounded.

'It must have moved,' he said, rather stupidly.

We spent three fruitless hours wandering around the hills of Tin Tehoun, until Hotan saw a kinsman of his in the distance and galloped off to ask him for directions. By the time we arrived at the camp, it was dark.

We did not enter alone. We were escorted in by an army of naked children. It was that juvenile happiness that I remember most about coming into the encampment. The laughing children crawled and screamed all over Hotan. Some of them were his own, others belonged to neighbours; it made no difference.

I slept well, until early in the morning, when I was awoken by the sound of water gushing out of a *guerba*. I jumped up with a sick feeling inside me and opened my eyes. It was only a sheep, who had escaped from a neighbour's enclosure and knocked over a *guerba*. I looked at the puddle of water complacently. There was a lot more from where that came.

Hotan's tent was far more 'African' than anything that I had seen at Chegga. It was made out of stretched skins, and next to the tent was an enclosure where Hotan's family kept their goats and sheep. Inside the tent the parched and dusty ground was covered by mats. In the middle sat Hotan's wife, breastfeeding her baby like a queen. She was hardly beautiful, but she had a certain presence about her and that silent strength that women who have to deal with weak husbands so often acquire.

I spent the morning eating a bulky meal that Hotan's wife had put before me and attending a morning surgery, arranged by Hotan for the benefit of his neighbours. After various wounds had been cleaned and bandaged, pain-killing tablets were given to the worthy sick, and salt tablets given to the unworthy.

I left with Hotan in mid-afternoon, bound for Timbuktu, two days away. I said goodbye to Hotan's wife and gave her half a dozen aspirins in gratitude for her hospitality. I looked for Lulai but could not find him. Hotan told me that he was sulking because he was not allowed to come to Timbuktu with us. We had only one camel now—the rest of the caravan was staying in the encampment with the salt—so we took it in turns to ride and walk.

As I had expected, Hotan's encampment was low on sugar. So before getting on the road to Timbuktu, we wandered off to the east in search of an old lady who reputedly had sugar for sale. She had none left, and directed us another five miles to the east, to another encampment. There for the cost of a hundred Malian francs (about ten pence) we were able to buy three tea glasses full of sugar. It was late. We decided to stop there for the night.

We had a New Year's Eve party of tea and mutton. An old lady without any teeth kept asking me if I had a radio, and cackled with laughter at every answer I gave. She was a friendly old hag; in a different culture she would have drunk neat gin. Whenever my mouth was empty, she tried to thrust a nomad pipe into it. She was the life and soul of the party. After we had eaten, I gave her some aspirins as a present. She promptly ran off to a nearby tent and exchanged them for a pouch of tobacco, which she gave to me, cackling away at my disjointed attempts of refusal.

1975 began with a bowl of camel's milk. Hotan wanted to stay at the tent for tea and food. But I bullied him into leaving. I knew that if we didn't leave before tea was brewed, we would never leave. He was silent and grumpy when we set off. After half a mile I relented. We stopped to drink tea and eat meat.

As we sat by the fire, brewing tea, a distantly-familiar shadow moved across the earth from the south. It was accompanied by a far-away roaring sound. I looked up. A jet plane was flying through the sky. It was the first plane that I had seen for a long time. Hotan got up and shouted, waving his arms in the air. But the plane couldn't see us. Tens of thousands of feet above us and tens of thousands of years ahead of us, we were not even specks.

The country that we were travelling through was rapidly changing. The grass was getting greener, the bushes were getting thicker, and nomad encampments were becoming more numerous. Hardly a mile went by without meeting someone or other. The only unpleasant aspect of the journey now was the cram-cram seeds. They covered the dry, dusty earth, clutching our hair, our clothes, and our skin, as we swept by.

At a Negro encampment about ten miles to the south of Tin Tehoun, we stopped by a fire to light a pipe of tobacco. They were a simple, generous people, warm and uncritical, with a natural courtesy that made me ashamed of my own standards.

> The negroes possess some admirable qualitites [wrote Ibn Battuta on his travels in the Soudan]. They are seldom unjust, and have a greater abhorrence of injustice than any other people.

Their sultan shows no mercy to anyone guilty of the least act of it. There is complete security in their country. Neither traveller nor inhabitant in it has anything to fear from robbers or men of violence. They do not confiscate the property of any white man [Arab] who dies in their country, even if it be uncounted wealth. On the contrary, they give it into the charge of some trustworthy person among the whites, until the rightful heir takes possession of it. They are careful to observe the hours of prayer, and assiduous in attending them in congregations, and in bringing up their children to them. . . . Among their bad qualitites are the following: the women servants, slave-girls, and young girls go about in front of everyone naked, without a stitch of clothing on them. Women go into the sultan's presence naked and without coverings, and his daughters also go about naked. Then there is their custom of putting dust and ashes on their heads as a mark of respect. . . . Another reprehensible practice among many of them is the eating of carrion, dogs, and asses. [4]

Finally we stopped at a depression in the hills, well sheltered by thorny bushes and scrubs. We lay down without lighting a fire. I could not sleep. Hotan could not sleep either. He was sitting on the ground cross-legged, with his blankets dropping down from his shoulders.

That was my last night before Timbuktu. I looked up at my old friend *Bel Hardi*, the North Star. I knew that I would never see it in quite the same light again. Then I looked at Hotan. I would not see him in the same light either.

'Hotan good guide, yes?'

'Yes, Hotan. You are a good guide . . . And a good man too.'

I could not bring myself to eat the next morning. The meat that Hotan's wife had given us was 'off'; perpetually surrounded by flies, it smelt disgusting. I told Hotan that I would only drink tea. He gave me a disappointed look. If I did not eat, then he would not eat. I tried to persuade him that he had every right to eat as much as he liked, but he was adamant. So the two of us ended up eating nothing.

[4] Battuta, *op. cit.*

Taking it in turns to ride the camel, we strolled on towards Timbuktu. On every hilltop I strained my eyes for the first sight of the city. As we rode and walked towards the last objective of our journey, we collected other travellers going in the same direction.

We passed a Tuareg with a pack camel. He was searching the ground for something that he had lost. When we came up to him, he ceased his search and joined us. We passed a man asleep in the middle of the track, with a goat tied to his ankle. When we stepped over him, the goat tried to bolt away. The man woke up and followed us with his goat. A little later a nomad woman stopped Hotan and asked him for some tobacco. He gave her some and she walked along beside us. We travelled over hills, along wadis, through light soft sand, and across flat stretches of woodland, passing the time swopping stories and experiences, like Chaucer's pilgrims on their way to Canterbury.

The first to sight Timbuktu was the man with the goat. He pointed to a high water-tower, its metal flashing in the afternoon sun.

'Timbuktu.'

'Timbuktu, *Hamdullah*.'

'*Hamdullah*.'

'*Ilhamdu Lillah. Ilhamdu Lillah*.'

We stopped for a moment on the crest of the hill and contemplated Timbuktu. There were smiles on all our faces. Only the two camels remained unimpressed. One place is very much the same as another to a camel.

We walked the last two miles. It was my turn to ride, but I felt awkward riding while the nomad woman walked. So I offered her my camel. She laughed, shaking her head in a refusal. The nomads around laughed in chorus. With unnecessary gallantry I became indignant. I said that I could not possibly ride while she walked, but that only made them laugh the more.

So we all ended up walking, with the *nasrani* leading a riderless camel. Thus the journey ended at Timbuktu the same way that it had begun at Chegga, on the edge of the ridiculous.

We came into the town over the communal rubbish dump, delicately picking our way through piles of old tin cans and abandoned cars, the symbols of the twentieth century.

Women of the Sahara

Women of Timbuktu

On guard in the Sahara

And then, beyond the rubbish dump and inside the gates of the city, I saw the men and women of the twentieth century, a whole street of them, with black, brown, and bronze faces. They stopped their work and stared. They did not stare in silence; they shouted and exclaimed in amazement at the dirty white man, dressed like a poor nomad, leading a riderless camel behind him. Above the noise I heard the hoot of a motor-car horn. A wave of movement swept through the crowd, and at once their faces turned towards a new object of attention. The crowd divided and an army jeep made its way through the opening. It stopped just in front of me. Three black soldiers got out and started walking towards me. The twentieth century was coming out to greet me. The lines of curious faces, the mass of vivid colour, were now silent. Then the twentieth century spoke out, in clear confident tones.

'*Monsieur*, you are under arrest.'

M

8

Timbuktu

We were escorted through the evening streets by the jeep to the Timbuktu military headquarters. It was a pretentious, dilapidated building in French colonial style. There I was taken before the Commandant who wore paratroop uniform and dark regulation sunglasses. He questioned me sharply about my visit to Taoudenni.

I acted the stupid Englishman.

After several minutes of pointless exchanges, he announced that I was no concern of his and sent me off, with a military escort, to the police headquarters on the other side of the main square.

With two soldiers on either side of me, I was taken across the Place de l'Indépendence with its statue of Pegasus ridden by a Tuareg. I could hear the sounds of Reggae music coming from the windows of a nearby government building.

> You can get it if you really want
> You can get it if you really want
> You can get it if you really want
> But you must try, try and try, try and try
> You'll succeed at last.[1]

It was bizarre.

The main police-station in Timbuktu had all the features of a sheriff's office in an Alabaman town. Inside the main door, a black kid of about fourteen years old was being questioned by a plain-clothes detective wearing an '007' buckle on his belt. A torn Smith and Wesson instruction poster, written in English, hung from a wall. A framed collage made up of newspaper photographs of Mali's 'Revolutionary Council' hung on the wall opposite.

[1] Jimmy Cliff, *You can get it if you really want*.

The plain-clothes policeman ordered the youth to be locked up. Then he took me down a corridor to the office of the Chief of Police. He knocked on the door and led me in. The Chief of Police sat opposite me, playing with a cigarette-lighter shaped like an automatic pistol.

'What were you doing crossing the desert?'

'Why did you go to Taoudenni?'

'Did you know that Taoudenni is a restricted military area?'

'Why did you spend so long in Taoudenni?'

Behind the Chief of Police an ancient pair of handcuffs hung down from a rack. A length of rubber hosepipe sat shamelessly on a filing cabinet to his right. Every time I tried to answer a question I was interrupted by another. In the end the Chief of Police accused me of being a spy and marched out of his office.

I was left alone with the detective who wore the '007' buckle. He let out a thin giggle and, pulling out a packet of Benson and Hedges, offered me one and took one for himself. He lit them both from the Police Chief's pistol-shaped cigarette-lighter and blew out an embittered little ring of smoke.

I had nothing to worry about, he told me with a make-believe smile. He himself was utterly convinced of my innocence. I was a tourist, he was sure of that. The problem was the Chief. He would be harder to convince. He produced a map and asked me to give him my exact route.

I complied.

'Trust me,' he said. 'I am a firm believer in justice and progress. You have nothing to fear from me.'

But in truth I did not trust him. I thought of his 'justice' and 'progress'. And the more I thought of them, the more distrustful I became. The Police Chief was only capable of brutality. This man was capable of cruelty.

The Police Chief came back and barked out an order. A few minutes later Hotan was brought into the office. He gave his usual ridiculous para-military salute, and stood beside me looking frightened.

'Fetch the Tamachek translator,' shouted the Police Chief.

'The man is not a Tuareg,' said '007' politely. 'He is an Arab.'

'Then fetch the Arabic translator.'

When the translator came in, Hotan began babbling excitedly in Arabic. He was saying something about a letter that the Commandant in Taoudenni had given him. The translator explained it to the Police Chief.

'Why didn't you produce it before?' screamed the Chief.

The translator repeated the question in Arabic.

'Because no one asked for it,' Hotan replied weakly.

The letter was produced and the Police Chief read it over carefully. Grudgingly he pronounced his judgement.

'You will be given a permit to stay here for eight days—no more. Before those eight days are up, you are to take a river-boat down the Niger to Gao, report to the police there, then take a camion up the Trans-Saharan Highway into Algeria. You are expressly forbidden to visit any other part of Mali. What you do when you get across the border into Algeria is your own affair.'

'The language of this region is Sungai [Songhai],' wrote Leo Africanus, 'the inhabitants are blacke and most friendly unto strangers.'[2]

Outside the police-station it was almost dark. Led by Hotan I made my way through the streets of Timbuktu to the house of Nagem, Hotan's son. He was at home. He welcomed us at his door and invited us both to stay in his house.

Nagem's house, with its ancient wooden door studded with iron bolts and delicately shaped wrought-iron window frames, was no different from any other house in Timbuktu. Inside was an open courtyard, surrounded by dark spacious rooms and cluttered with mats, blankets, cooking utensils, and fly-covered babies.

Nagem ould Hotan had come a long way from the encampment at Tin Tehoun. He was a soldier in the Malian Army and could speak French. He was a pleasant, informed, and cheerful man, with a distinctly unmilitary air about him. When we knocked on his door, he was in the middle of changing out of khaki fatigues into traditional nomad clothes.

[2] Africanus, *op. cit.*, Vol. III.

We drank tea and ate meat and rice with our fingers. After the
meal, Nagem presented me with a packet of cigarettes.

That evening a policeman knocked on his door to inquire
after me. Nagem went out to talk to him and came back looking
very embarrassed.

'It is very awkward,' he said. 'I am a soldier and you are a
foreigner.'

The policeman had told him that I had to stay in the town's
only hotel, where, no doubt, the authorities could keep an eye on
me. But Nagem had offered me hospitality for the night and an
Arab does not go back on his word. Tomorrow I must leave his
house and go into the hotel.

'It is politics,' he said with a regretful smile. I told him that I
understood.

I woke up late the next morning, and it was not until midday that
I had washed, deloused myself, shaved off my two-month beard,
and changed into shirt and jeans. It was the first time that I had
worn trousers since leaving Tindouf.

I left Nagem's house to stroll around the city. More than anything else, Timbuktu had the aura of a decaying port, with the
sea, in the form of sand, coming up into the streets; a caravan
of salt being unloaded in a side street looked like a convoy of
ships, and the Arabs in their long billowing robes sailed by as if
they were wearing spinnakers. Renaissance Venice must have
looked something like this. And as in all ports, there was an
extraordinary combination of cultures, customs, and costumes.

There were Arabs squatting around street-corner fires brewing
tea, Tuaregs in veils moving around the streets with an air of
superiority, Mandigo traders, tall and unmistakable in their long
robes and red fezes, carrying goatskins full of water on their
shoulders.

If that Arab influence was strongest in the two great mosques,
the Jingerber and the Sankore, the only two historic monuments
that Timbuktu can boast of, then the negro influence was
strongest in Timbuktu's teeming, sweaty market-place. Here
obese Songhai mammas, with strong bulging muscles, black
polished shoulders, and long drooping breasts, sold fish and

water melons—laughing, shouting and ragging, their cheap
gaudy dresses and beautiful butch faces reminding me of a line
from a poem by Nicki Giovanni, 'My feet have seen more than
your eyes will ever read'.

The city had changed a great deal since Leo Africanus's famous
description of Timbuktu, written four hundred years ago.

> Here are many shops of artificers and merchants, and especially
> of such as weave linnen and cotton cloth. And hither do the
> Barbaric merchants bring clothe of Europe. All the women
> of this region except the main-servants go with their faces
> covered, and sell all necessarie victuals. The inhabitants, and
> especially strangers there residing, are exceedingly rich, inso-
> much that the king that now is, married both his daughters
> unto two rich merchants. Here are many wels containing most
> sweete water; and so often as the river Niger overfloweth they
> conveigh the water thereof by certain sluces into the towne.
> Corne, cattle, milk and butter this region yeeldeth in great
> abundance: but salt is verie scarce heere, for it is brought
> hither by land from Tegaza which is five hundred miles
> distant. . . .
>
> The inhabitants are people of a gentle and cheerful dis-
> position, and spend a great part of the night in singing and
> dancing through all the streets of the citie; they keep great
> store of men and women-slaves, and their town is much in
> danger of fire: at my second being there halfe the town almost
> was burnt in fivee howers' space. Without the suburbs there
> are no gardens nor orchards at all. . . .
>
> Here are greate store of doctors, judges, priests, and other
> learned men, that are bountifully maintained at the king's cost
> and charges. And hither are brought divers manuscripts or
> written books out of Barbarie, which are sold for more money
> than any other merchantise. The coin of Tombuto is of gold
> without any stampe or superscription: but in matters of smal
> value they use certain shels brought hither out of the kingdom
> of Persia. [3]

[3] Africanus, *op. cit.*, Vol. III.

Leo, of course, was describing Timbuktu at the peak of its power and prosperity. It was just the description a fascinated Europe wanted. For centuries Timbuktu had been no more than an idea. Though no one in Europe knew exactly where it was, no one doubted that it was a great metropolis. To Christians it was the mythical kingdom of Prester John; to merchants it was a great centre of commerce with roofs made of gold; to politicians it was the capital of a great Central African empire; and to scholars it was a place of learning that hid priceless manuscripts that would solve the mysteries of an age.

Leo also mentioned 'cottages built of chalk and covered with thatch', but nobody wanted to know.

By the time a young Frenchman dressed in Arab clothing arrived in the city, three centuries after Leo, Timbuktu was but a shadow of its former glory.

'I looked around and found that the sight before me did not answer my expectations. I had formed a totally different idea of the grandeur and wealth of Timbuktu.'

René Caillié was totally disillusioned.

The city presented, at first sight, nothing but a mass of ill-looking houses built of earth. Nothing was seen in all directions but immense plains of quicksand of a yellowish-white colour. The sky was pale red as far as the horizon: all nature wore a dreary aspect, and the most profound silence prevailed; not even the warbling of a bird was to be heard. Still, though I cannot account for the impression, there was something imposing in the aspect of a great city raised in the midst of sands, and the difficulties surmounted by its founders cannot fail to excite admiration. [4]

News of my arrival had spread through the city, particularly among the Berebish, who had heard about me from the caravan crews who had overtaken us. I was an object of curiosity and felt among friends. Wherever I went I was greeted with the cry 'Hey, rajel Taoudenni' (Hey, Taoudenni man).

Dusk was coming down. There was one more place to visit.

[4] Caillié, op. cit., Vol. II.

It was almost a pilgrimage. I walked through the market-place, and down a series of narrow streets that led to the French-built Lyceé. Just before I reached the Lyceé, I stopped outside a simple house made of mud and plaster. Above the door was a bronze plaque.

'René Caillié. 1828'

I stood for a while outside the house, almost in awe. Caillié had not been the first European to reach Timbuktu (the first was a Scotsman, Major Gordon Laing, who had lived in a house opposite Caillié's), but it was Caillié with whom I identified. Like Caillié I had travelled to Timbuktu almost impoverished; like Caillié I had been the object of ridicule and suspicion; and like Caillié I had no official permission for being here. He was neither an imperialist, nor a missionary, nor a trader, just a vagabond like myself. I could not have wished for a better hero.

It was evening. I made my way to Nagem's house to collect my belongings and take them to the hotel. Hotan helped me to carry them. It was a sad moment when we reached the hotel and put my saddle-bag, sleeping-bag, and map case down onto the bed.

I gave Hotan my extra pair of sandals and entrusted to him my Ridiculous Knife of Heroic Proportions to give to Lulai. Then I offered him my hand.

'The peace of God be with you,' I said to him.

He did not take my outstretched hand; instead he clasped my shoulders and kissed me on both cheeks. As the tears swelled in my eyes, his kind and simple face lost its outlines and blurred out of focus. There had been times when I had hated him, despised him, patronized him, and considered him the lowest of the low. But in that one gesture and in the look that accompanied it, there was more humanity and simple human decency that anything that I had ever encountered. I turned away, embarrassed at the tears that were rolling down my face. I could hear him shuffling out of the door in his bare feet. When I looked up the room was empty.

I went out onto the hotel patio, listening to the sinking and swelling of African drums far away, their weird, suggestive rhythm sending tremors through my body. Inside the hotel manager's office, a record of James Brown was put onto the gramophone.

I tried to go back over my journey, but I couldn't. I caught an image here, grabbed an incident there like pieces of a jigsaw puzzle, but they were nothing put together but pieces from a larger jigsaw puzzle that would take time and distance to collect and fit together. And even that jigsaw puzzle was only part of a larger one that would include all those djinns from my past, and represent an even longer journey.

The record of James Brown came to an end and the door of the hotel bar opened. A shaft of light came across the patio. Inside the bar I could hear American accents. I suddenly realized how long it had been since I had heard English voices. I went into the bar and ordered a beer. The Americans at their table invited me to join them. They were petroleum explorers; their work was almost over, they told me.

After a while one of them asked me what my name was.

I told him.

The oilmen looked at me with accusing silence.

'Christ,' one of them said. 'We had given you up for dead. We've had two Land-Rovers out looking for you for the last two weeks.'

I felt a fool, but it didn't matter. My thoughts went back to Tindouf, to the Sous-Préfet and his shadow of a shadow of a smile. Now I knew what it was that he had almost told me, now I shared the secret that he shared, I understood what lay 'beyond sound of voice or movement of the tongue'. And as I listened to the oilmen telling me how the British Foreign Office in London had telegrammed the British Embassy in Dakar, how the British Embassy in Dakar had telegrammed the American Embassy in Bamako, and how the American Embassy in Bamako had radioed the American oilmen in Timbuktu, I could almost see that shadow of a shadow of a smile.

A Revolt in the Desert

A Revolt in the Desert

I returned to Tindouf a little over a year after my arrival at Timbuktu. The week that I spent there must have been one of the saddest weeks of my life. Tindouf had changed almost beyond recognition. Everywhere there were troops, tanks, MiG fighters and anti-aircraft guns.

It was not only Tindouf that had changed, the actual desert had changed too. All along the Hammada, from Tindouf to the Moroccan frontier, great fortifications were being built. And along the approaches to Tindouf were new sand-dunes, shaped neither by the wind nor the dictates of God, but by military bulldozers and the dictates of the Algerian Army's Corps of Engineering.

And the people had gone through changes too, from proud and unhumbled nomads into confused and humiliated refugees, mere shadows of themselves. Then they had changed again, the shadows rediscovered themselves, and a new man was beginning to make his appearance in the Sahara Desert, the revolutionary socialist nomad, still 'turbulent, predatory, elusive, and unassailable', but with something else, something that he had never had before: a vision.

For War, that terrible man-made plague, had swept across the western Sahara, first across the Spanish Sahara, then into southern Morocco, northern Mauritania, and western Algeria. And the long lines of caravans that had drifted south each winter like birds, had finally ceased their migration.

How had it happened?

In mid-October 1975, in defiance of the United Nations, the Organization for African Unity, and the International Court of Justice in The Hague, King Hassan of Morocco assembled a 350,000-strong 'peaceful' army, pledged to 'liberate' the Spanish Sahara.

Spain found herself in an impossible position. Her main ally, the United States, supported Morocco, her head of state, Franco, lay dying, and her internal political state was uncertain.

For a moment it had looked as if the western Sahara would be defended. Spain reinforced her garrisons, Algeria moved troops up to the Moroccan border, Juan Carlos flew to el Aaiun to stiffen the morale of the Spanish Army, the United Nations Secretary-General called for a six-months 'cooling-off' period, and the Polisario Front, who had rapidly gained strength since I had left the Sahara, announced that they would resist the Moroccans with force.

That moment did not last. Hassan announced that the 'Green March' would go ahead (although without him leading it, as he had previously promised) and on 6 November 1975, his 'peaceful' army, led by tanks and covered by jet fighters and bombers, crossed the Saharan frontier. Eight days later a tripartite agreement was signed between Spain, Morocco, and Mauritania. The Spanish Sahara was to be divided between the two leading contestants, Morocco and Mauritania, with Morocco taking the lion's share, including the 1700 tons of phosphate deposits at Bu Craa. At no time in the tripartite discussions was the will of the people of the Sahara, the Saharauis, ever seriously considered. This was somewhat unrealistic. The Saharauis had no intention of having Spanish rulers replaced by Moroccan and Mauritanian ones. The majority favoured independence. They wanted the Sahara to be Saharaui, as the Spanish on the radio had promised them it always would be.

In the event the Spanish withdrew, and it was left to the Polisario and their nomad allies to resist the new colonialists with force. The bulk of the nomads who fought with the Polisario were Rguibat, like the ones I had met at Chegga on my way to Taoudenni. They were a warlike people, who called themselves 'the sons of the cloud' and were the largest tribe in the western Sahara. They were joined by other tribes who came by lorry, camel and foot from northern Mauritania, western Algeria, and northern Mali to join them. But their ancient rifles and ancient standards of chivalry were no match against Moroccan tanks and heavy artillery. By the end of November, el Aaiun the political

capital, Semara the cultural capital, and Bu Craa the phosphate
mine were occupied. As the Moroccans came down from the
north, so the Mauritanians came up from the south, sweeping
before them thousands of refugees, fleeing from the invading
armies towards Tindouf, on the other side of the Iguidi Desert,
where refugee camps had been built by the Algerians. By the
time I arrived at Tindouf in March, there was only one area in the
former Spanish Sahara that was still resisting the invaders, el
Guelta, a mountainous plateau in the centre of the territory,
hemmed in by the Moroccans to the north and the Mauritanians
to the south.

Nor was it just the political and military landscape that had
changed. I had changed too. The Sous-Préfet, Omar, Dermas,
the Half-Child, Hotan, even the Commandant of Taoudenni, had
left their marks on me. I found London a dull, dreary place, and I
felt alienated from old friends. They measured all cultures by the
standards of their own and could not comprehend my admiration
for illiterate male chauvinist pigs, nor could they comprehend the
security that comes from having nothing left to lose. Long periods
of silence and a yearning to return are what I remember most
about that year, and a feeling of homelessness. Some of my friends
accepted this, others patronized me as a curiosity, a few found me
a bore.

And so when the chance arrived, thanks to the *Observer*, to
return to Tindouf, I seized the opportunity without reservation.
When I arrived I was shocked. A few miles away from the town,
on what had once been empty desert, there were forty thousand
refugees, between fifty and seventy per cent of the Saharaui
population, according to *Le Monde*. It was the greatest gathering
of Saharauis ever recorded.

They lived in a vast city of tents that stretched for acres over
the stones and sand. They called the camp 'Hafid-Boudjemma',
after one of the first Polisario leaders to be killed. The city had no
centre; its inhabitants seemed to object to the idea of centralized
government. Hafid-Boudjemma was more a collection of
hundreds of nomad encampments of between ten and twenty
tents each, than a metropolis. It was a city of suburbs without a

centre. Every so often, among the brown and dark blue low-lying Saharan tents, could be seen the square, blue-coloured tents of the Algerian Red Crescent. From these tents the wounded were cared for and the relief food was distributed. Caring for the refugees was a gigantic operation. Food and medical supplies alone cost the Algerian Government £25,000 a day.

My destination was el Guelta, the last area under Polisario control. For over a year, since the Spanish Army had withdrawn from their outposts there, the region had been administered by the 'Councils of Forty', the old pre-colonial structure of government. Now el Guelta was crammed with thousands of refugees who had been unable to make the terrible journey to Tindouf. Not only was the Moroccan Army in positions to the north of el Guelta, but their troops had occupied large areas of northern Mauritania, cutting off el Guelta from the bulk of the Polisario, at Tindouf. A Moroccan attack on el Guelta was expected daily, and a relief column was collecting at Hafid-Boudjemma to cross the Iguidi Desert by night, bringing supplies in and taking the refugees out. I had secured myself a place on the column, and was in Hafid-Boudjemma waiting to leave.

'We cannot tell you the exact day that you will leave,' said the Polisario officer who had shown me to the tent where I would be staying. 'You must have your bags packed each night and be ready. One night I will come up to you and say "Today we leave". Then we leave.'

'*Inshallah*,' I said.

'*Inshallah*,' he replied.

Each night I had my bags packed, ready to leave. And each night I waited for him to come and say 'Today we leave'. But he never came.

But I did not waste the time I spent waiting. I used those days to rediscover the Saharan nomad, for a rediscovery it was. These people had changed since I had last seen them. They had rediscovered themselves.

I was aware of this change from the moment that I entered the camp. For the first time nomad women, dressed in their blue and black, looked me straight in the face and answered me back. Their children now attended make-shift schools, marked by no

A Polisario flying column in search of cigarettes

Three former Moroccan soldiers, now Polisario revolutionaries

A woman in her place

more than a circle of stones on the sand, where they were learning the three 'r's' (reading, writing, 'rithmetic and revolution), and forever reciting their slogan 'The Sahara is Saharaui', like verses of the Koran. But the greatest change of all was amongst the Blacks. They no longer regarded themselves as social inferiors, and sat unself-consciously on the mats next to their ex-masters.

And everywhere there was the drone of the transistor radio.

The Moroccan-Mauritanian invasion, the displacement of a population, and the great social upheaval that followed it, had worked to destroy Tahar Omar's delicately balanced social ladder, leaving amid the broken rungs what must be one of the most democratic and tightly-knit societies in the world. For the very inhospitality of the desert around, which had given the nomads their sense of individualism and self-reliance, had given them communal loyalties and survival instincts that bound each to the other so firmly that only death could break the bond.

I remember asking one Polisario officer whether these people, perhaps the most individualistic people in the world, would ever make 'good communists'.

'People who share their last litre of water when they are a hundred kilometres from a well are already half-way to becoming "good communists",' he snapped back.

That particular Polisario officer had been educated at Madrid University. He had read all the standard revolutionary books, from Karl Marx to Franz Fanon, and he had attended all the right anti-Facist demonstrations at the University. But the standards that he set himself were not the standards of the European revolutionary. His standards were those of the nomad. His socialism was not the highly complex socialism of Europe, but a simple socialism based on the nomads' own lifestyle. He had no books to consult this time; the experiment of socialism among the Saharan nomads had never been tried before. Karl Marx wasn't much use in the Sahara.

'When I came here,' he told me later, 'I thought that it would be me that was teaching the nomads. The longer I stay here, the more I realize that it is they who are teaching me.'

He was not the only one with those feelings. Most of the young 'politicos' had gone through the same experience. They moved

N

around the camp looking like a cross between Tolstoyian idealists and political commissioners with tendencies towards bourgeois individualism. From a distance, in their camouflaged robes, they looked the same as the ordinary nomads. Close-up, you could spot the difference. Underneath their desert-coloured *jelabas*, the 'politicos' wore jeans.

The refugees from the towns had gone through the same kind of experiences. They might have lived in the towns for generations, but they used the standards of the nomad as their own. Though they boasted of Honda motor-bikes and transistor radios, they saw in those wild and illiterate people of the desert a model for all men. Their flight across the Iguidi Desert must have been a terrifying experience. Hundreds died from hunger, thirst, bombs, and napalm. The routes they took, from La Guara, Villa Cisneros, el Aaiun, and Marbes, were littered with bodies and possessions abandoned on the way.

'I left my home with my family on the night that the Moroccans arrived,' a taxi-driver from Villa Cisneros told me. 'The Spanish soldiers had orders to stop us leaving, but when we came up to their road-blocks, they looked the other way. For two days we drove across the desert. All along the route were lines of refugees. On the third day we ran out of petrol. For the last two days we walked.

'We went first to the mountains of Guelta, where Moroccan planes bombed us every day. They came in regularly at five o'clock in the afternoon. At first everyone panicked and ran into the rocks and caves, where many people were killed. After a while we learnt to lie in the soft sand with yellow tarpaulins over us. I was evacuated from Guelta in a Red Crescent lorry a week ago.'

I give these words unedited and without reservation. I make no claim to neutrality. For a short but significant period of my life these people had given me a home. The bonds that tied me to them were strong. The nomads of the Sahara no more expected me to be neutral than I would have expected Omar to be neutral if we had been attacked by bandits.

And Omar? Dermas? The others? What happened to them? I just don't know. Every day I searched Tindouf and the refugee camp for their faces. Every day I asked about them. But I never found them.

I remember one day, in a Red Crescent tent, asking the doctor if he had heard of Omar. He looked at me as if I was mad.

'There are nearly 50,000 people here. Do you expect me to have the names of them all. Some of them are children who have lost their parents. And some of them do not even have names.'

The only concrete piece of news I could get was about the Half-Child and the Sous-Préfet. The Half-Child was now at school in Tindouf, and the Sous-Préfet had been transferred to another district in the north of Algeria. I hope that neither of them are too unhappy in their new worlds.

Yet although I could not find any old friends, I was not lonely. Everywhere I went strangers came up to me and told me how glad they were that I had come back.

I remember another visit to the Red Crescent tents. I was talking to a Spanish girl who had volunteered as a nurse.

'Here there are sufficient medicines,' she said, 'but in the camps inside the territory there is a shortage of everything.'

'What is most urgently needed?'

'An end to the bombing.'

In the corner of the tent I could see a result of that bombing. She was lying on her stomach with her head to one side. Her lovely aquiline face suggested a girl about fifteen years old. Her long, slender back was a distortion of burns and bubbles.

The smell of the ether was overpowering. I went outside to breathe some fresh air. In a nearby tent the evening meal was being prepared. An old man, the head of the household, beckoned me over.

'*Aggi, aggi.*' ('Come here, come here'.)

I went up to him and together we went through the salutations.

'Are you the *nasrani* who went to Taoudenni?' he asked me.

I said I was.

'You are our friend. Come and eat.'

The next day a young man stopped outside my tent. He had a bearded face of indeterminate appearance. I invited him in and he sat down opposite me. He spoke for a while to some Libyans who were in the tent, then he turned to me. We exchanged courtesies, and in the long period of silence that followed (long periods of silence are never embarrassing among nomads) he studied me. After several minutes of silence and platitudes, we moved on to talking politics. I put the usual political questions to him, but the replies that I got were unusual. He seemed to be better informed than most of the 'politicos' that I spoke to, and had more confidence. His description of how the Polisario had been born in the universities, spread in the towns, and finally found itself in the desert, was all first-hand. He gave me an impressive political analysis of the situation, with a nomad's ability to get down to essentials.

'King Hassan's claim to a "Greater Morocco" is not what this war is about,' he said. 'It is about the price of phosphates. If Morocco can control the mines at Bu Craa, then she will have a monopoly of the phosphate market.' (Just as the Moroccan ruling class sought to enrich themselves by controlling the price of salt and gold, now they enrich themselves by controlling the price of phosphates, I thought.) 'They will find it hard. Our liberty is worth more than a few stones.'

I found him intelligent and capable, and I wondered who he was. It wasn't until he had left the tent that I was able to ask the Libyans his name.

'Oh, that was Sayed.'

'Sayed who?'

'Mustapha Sayed.'

'Mustapha Sayed who?'

'El Oueli Mustapha Sayed.'

That was how I met el Oueli, founder, leader, and Secretary-General of the Polisario Front.

I met him again that afternoon, and we wandered together for a while through the cluster of tents that grew out of the stony desert around us. Everywhere we went, he was constantly stopped by nomads asking for his advice and his judgement. He seemed to dislike this role, and wherever possible he got the nomads to solve their own problems, but it was an uphill battle. The camp was entirely administered by the Polisario, and since the nomads saw el Oueli as one of the leaders of the Polisario, it was inevitable that they should come to him. Political admini-

strations among nomads have always been intensely individualistic, their effectiveness depending on the degree of respect that
each ruler can command. El Oueli may have disliked this personal
system of government—it did not fit in with his socialist and
revolutionary ideas—but to the nomads it was comprehensible
and human, and far fairer than an administration of faceless
bureaucrats whom they would despise.

And so, for the first time, I witnessed a revolutionary nomad
government in action. Somebody's goats had been stolen, a
child was missing, there was a dispute over some family's
property. When el Oueli wanted me to understand his answers,
he spoke in clear, simple Arabic; when he didn't, he rattled off
his answers in a broad, incomprehensible Hassaniya. It was the
simplest and surest form of political censorship I had come across.

Suddenly we saw a Land-Rover racing up to us. It was swerving
through the tents to avoid the guy-ropes. It skidded to a halt. A
'politico' jumped out and ran up to el Oueli. He spoke to el
Oueli, who shouted out his apologies to me, jumped into the
Land-Rover, and roared off.

That was the last I saw of el Oueli. Three months later he was
dead, shot while leading an attack on Nouakschott, according to
one report, killed in a skirmish with Mauritanian troops near el
Guelta, according to a second, assassinated by Algerian secret
service agents, according to a third.

That evening, at el Oueli's suggestion, I attended one of those
nightly political meetings that are a compulsory activity in every
revolutionary upsurge. I arrived early to make sure I secured a
place. The sun was settling down over the western world and the
inhabitants of the tent were saying their evening prayers. I
waited outside the tent in silence.

At the end of the prayers I was welcomed with tea and
cigarettes. The master of the tent, who had had some contact
with the towns, spoke to me in a mixture of Spanish and French.
It was difficult to understand. I knew no more than half a dozen
words in Spanish. He seemed to think that the two languages
were the same.

Night grew darker, and the tent began to fill up. As more

people came in, so the camel-haired walls of the tent bulged that much more. Each time it looked as if not another limb would fit in; then a dozen more nomads would squeeze themselves into the tent.

After the speeches there was a further outburst of pushing and shoving. A space was cleared in the centre of the tent and four men walked in. I had never seen nomads like this before. Their matted curly hair exploded around their heads like Afros. Their clothes were gaudier and more colourful than those of the other nomads, and they had about them an apartness that reminded me of the Romany people in Europe.

These four men were '*iggauen*', my neighbour told me, tribeless wandering minstrels who made their living by singing, dancing, and telling stories in nomad encampments. They were good fellows, I was told, but unreliable and untrustworthy—just like gypsies, in fact.

While three of them took out their musical instruments, a drum, a guitar and a tambourine, the fourth sat down cross-legged in the middle of the tent, and in a low, monotonous voice began to tell a story. It was a familiar story by now, the nomads gathering in the west, the tanks coming down from the north, and the inevitable slaughter.

> They hungered, they thirsted,
> And though they were few,
> They fought like many.
> For they fought to live free,
> Or at least die in liberty.

As the song-story went on, so the three musicians began to accompany it, with the audience taking up the refrain at the end of each verse.

> For they fought to live free,
> Or at least die in liberty.

Soon the song reached the present, with el Guelta and Tindouf figuring in the lines. Suddenly its tempo quickened and the song moved into the future. The story-teller was up on his feet, jumping, twisting and turning in a frenzied war-dance. He moved faster and faster as the flickering half-light of the cheap paraffin lamp cast distorted shadows on the tent's walls.

Two Saharaui women then got up and began to dance with him. The audience roared with approval, clapping their hands and swaying their bodies in time with the music. As the story-teller began cutting the air with his sword, so the two women dancers took over the centre of the stage, becoming one in their movements, their bodies shaking and their bangles jangling. They seemed totally unaware of their surroundings, totally taken over by the powerful rhythm of the music. Even as their clothes began to fall off their heads, they paid no heed. Their veils fell from around their faces, revealing thick black hair wound in complex braids around their head-pieces; their robes dropped from their shoulders, revealing soft, blue-tinted shoulders, and their breasts, hardly covered by the folds of their robes, shook with the music. Finally they collapsed onto the ground, their bodies shivering with tension and bathed in sweat.

By now the tent was so crowded that not even the three musicians could move. Yet that deterred nobody. The whole gathering began to dance spontaneously, those who could not fit inside, spilling outside.

It was a powerful sight. These were no hybrid bums, dancing and making fools of themselves in front of goggle-eyed tourists. Their ancestors, the Almovids, had conquered most of Spain, the Sahara, and the Soudan. Some of these dancers had been at Nouadhibou, when the tiny but tough Mauritanian army had taken on the Polisario. There had been ten days of bitter fighting before the Polisario abandoned the town. Others had fought against the Moroccans in the north, their battles as hopeless as they were heroic. Most of them had been bombed by napalm, many were barefooted, and some possessed nothing but the rags they stood up in.

It was well into the small hours of the morning when the dancing finally finished. I made my way back to my tent alone. A dog barked out of the blackness. A family row had reached its climax nearby. Somewhere in that city of tents, a woman lamented the death of a husband, her wailing rising and falling through the stillness of the night. It was the wailing of acceptance, not of grief. Hour after hour she called on her god for strength, but the darkness brought no comfort and the cold wind no relief.

They are a people of primary colours [wrote the Englishman T. E. Lawrence], especially black and white, who see the world always in line. They are a certain people, despising doubt, our modern crown of thorns. They do not understand our metaphysical difficulties, our self-questionings. They know only truth and untruth, belief and unbelief, without our hesitating retinue of finer shades. . . .

Their thoughts live easiest among extremes. They inhabit superlatives by choice. Sometimes the great inconsistencies seem to possess them jointly. They exclude compromise, and pursue the logic of their ideas to its absurd ends, without seeing incongruity in their opposed conclusions. . . .

They show no longing for great industry, no organizations of mind or body anywhere. They invent no systems of philosophy or mythologies. They are the least morbid of peoples, who take the gift of life unquestioning, as an axiom. To them it is a thing inevitable, entailed on man, as usufruct, beyond our control. Suicide is a thing nearly impossible and death no grief.

They are a people of spasms, of upheavals, of ideas, the race of the individual genius. Their movements are the more shocking by contrast with the quietude of every day, their great men greater by contrast with the humanity of their mass.[1]

A few days later I left Hafid-Boudjemma camp for another Polisario encampment close to the Mauritanian frontier. We travelled through the desert in a stripped-down Santyana Land-Rover that the driver raced across the desert floor as if it was a go-cart. The camp was smaller than Hafid-Boudjemma, but had a more military appearance. There I met three Moroccan soldiers who had deserted to the Polisario eight days earlier. Still wearing their Moroccan Army uniforms, they claimed that the Moroccan Army stayed mostly in the towns. The desert was 'bled as-siba',

[1] T. E. Lawrence, Intro. to *Travels in Arabia Deserts* by C. M. Doughty, London, 1921.

the unfriendly country. The Saharaui Polisario accepted them readily, like honoured guests. Nor were they the only non-Saharauis there. I met Spanish, Moroccan, and Mauritanian left-wingers, not to mention the scores of nomads who did not claim to belong to any country at all.

By the time I returned to Hafid-Boudjemma it was dark. I had one more call to make that night, to el Amine Mohammed, Prime Minister of the recently proclaimed Saharan Democratic Republic, a republic that existed nowhere but in the minds of the people at Tindouf and el Guelta. He was sitting cross-legged in a tent, dressed like the nomads who were with him. It wasn't until he was pointed out to me that I realized that he was the Prime Minister. He was only a few years older than me, young for a Prime Minister. He was a hard man, with an uncompromising message.

'We are fighting for more than our rights to liberty and independence—rights recognized by the United Nations and the entire international community—we are fighting for our very existence. It is because the United Nations was unable to ensure us these rights that we took the matter into our own hands. We have taken arms and proclaimed our republic, and we will continue our just struggle until victory, no matter how long it takes.'

I took my leave and went outside. Close-by, three stripped-down Land-Rovers were preparing to go out into the desert. For each Land-Rover there was a crew of six men, wearing khaki robes and turbans, and armed with AK47s (given to them by the Algerian and Libyan governments). One of them had some verses of the Koran tied around his neck. The Flying columns of the Long Range Desert Group in World War II must have looked something like this, though less spectacular and less tragic. As they sat in their Land-Rovers waiting to go, the driver of the lead vehicle lit a cigarette. I could see his face in the glow of the match. There was a familiar look to that face, I had seen it before. I had seen it on Dermas during those thirsty days before Taoudenni. It was the face of a man who was not yet ready to give up.

Presently an officer gave an order and the three Land-Rovers drove off into the darkness. 'Men travel by night,' that saintly

rebel Hussien said, before being pierced in the lips by a spear,
'and meet their destiny coming towards them, and that, I know,
is Death.'

Two days later I was driven into Tindouf to meet the third of
the Polisario's three leaders, Baba Miské Mohammed. I had
heard about him the last time I was in the Sahara—indeed, it was
hard not to have heard of him in the Sahara—and I was anxious
to meet him before I left for el Guelta. He was an exceptional
person. A Saharaui nobleman and a brilliant politician, he had
served Mauritania in three capacities: as her ambassador at the
United Nations, as a leader of her left-wing opposition, and as a
political prisoner. Later he went into exile, living in Paris where
he became the editor of the left-wing review *Afrique-Asia*. In the
last year he had returned to the Sahara and joined the Polisario.
He was one of the Polisario's best assets, the most sophisticated
and experienced politician in the movement, and the only one
with an international political reputation.

More than any other figure in the Polisario, he had been
subjected to a vile campaign of slander and character assassination,
unprecedented even by North African standards. According to
the Moroccan and Mauritanian radios, he was a Mauritanian
traitor, a renegade who had sold his country for Algerian and
Russian gold, an evil man who would not rest until he saw the
Sahara plunged into anarchy. But according to his friends and
admirers, he was the most noble of men, a nomad, born in the
Sahara, who went to New York to represent the cause of the
Sahara, a man who abandoned a spectacular political career
for the cause he believed in.

When I met him, he was wearing a blue Saharaui *bou-bou*
(sleeveless robe) and his face was semi-covered in an indigo-blue
turban. He was about forty years old, with a squat face and
pointed beard. He had Omar's tight cunning eyes, and the
Sous-Préfet's intelligent and ironic smile.

He answered the slanders that had been thrown against him
with dignity and humour.

'I am not, and I never have been, a Mauritanian. I am a
Saharaui. It is true that I spent a period of my life in Mauritania;
it is true that I have represented Mauritania and worked in

Mauritania. But I am no more a Mauritanian than a Palestinian who goes to work in Saudi Arabia is a Saudi. It is really very funny that at the very moment when Mauritania is declaring that Mauritania and the Sahara are one, she should accuse me, a Saharaui, of being a Mauritanian agitator among the Saharaui.'

Later we talked politics. He was impressive, with a pragmatism combined with breadth of vision. Talking to him, Saharan socialism seemed conceivable, and, he warned me, more was at stake than just the Sahara.

'This war could act as a catalyst throughout the whole Magreb. The Mauritanians, with their racial and cultural links with the Saharauis, are against the war and fear Morocco's expansionist aims. The government is weak, and the break could come at any time. In Morocco, the situation is different; the government is more firmly entrenched. But there are weak spots. The longer the war, the greater the disillusionment in the country. The King is gambling on a quick victory, and time is not on his side.'

Listening to him talk, I couldn't help thinking of the Englishman Erskine Childers. Both men had discarded spectacular political careers to fight against their ex-colleagues, both had been subjected to campaigns of libel and slander, both had fought against their own adopted country for principles that they believed in. Childers's end was in front of a firing squad. I hope and pray that Baba Miské's will not be so tragic.

That day, while I had been talking to Baba Miské, el Guelta had fallen. We heard the news next morning. There would be no convoy now. I wanted to stay, but I knew that I would not be able to. I was little use to these people, except to write it all down, and that could be done in London. There was nothing to do but go home—wherever that now was.

The plane did not leave until mid-afternoon. That morning the camp of Hafid-Boudjemma was very subdued. The news of the defeat at el Guelta had quickly spread through the tents. Hafid-Boudjemma was silent and tense. Soon the mourning would begin. The Polisario drove me back to Tindouf in one of their Land-Rovers. We drove in silence. There was nothing to say. The fall of el Guelta was not only a severe political and psychological defeat, it was also a serious military defeat. It was the only base that the Polisario had inside the territory. It would be a long time before another one could be established.

I arrived in Tindouf with over two hours to spare before I caught the plane for Algiers. I climbed onto the Hammada. It was the same spot that I had climbed eighteen months earlier, before leaving with Tahar Omar for Taoudenni. As I looked out over Tindouf and the desert for the last time, a terrible sadness overwhelmed me: sadness for the refugees and the Polisario trapped at el Guelta, probably dying at that very moment; sadness for the refugees at Hafid-Boudjemma, 'vice-regents of the earth' who would almost inevitably end up as second-rate Palestinians; and sadness for myself, who had come to the Sahara and for a brief moment had thought he had found a home, only to return and find it lying shattered all around him.

Index